I0531205

Reconstructing Faith: 365 Days to Reconsider Jesus
© 2026 by Dick Daniels

All rights reserved under International Copyright Law.
Contents and/or cover may not be reproduced
in whole or in part in any form without the express
written consent of the publisher.

Hardcover ISBN: 979-8-9908193-7-5
Paperback ISBN: 979-8-9908193-8-2
ePub ISBN: 979-8-9908193-9-9

Leadership Development Group

Cover and interior design:
The Brand Office

THE365DAYLEADER.ORG

RECONSTRUCTING
FAI+H

365 DAYS
to Reconsider Jesus

DR. DICK DANIELS

THE LEADERSHIP DEVELOPMENT GROUP

ALSO BY THE AUTHOR

Two nationally awarded collections are available at your favorite online bookstore in hardcover, paperback, Audible, and Kindle formats.

THE LEADERSHIP DEVELOPMENT GROUP LIBRARY by Dick Daniels
The series built on the assumption that leadership is a learned competency.

Leadership Briefs: Shaping Organizational Culture to Stretch Leadership Capacity *Midwest Book Award Gold Medallion for Business Books and Reader Views Reviewers Choice Award*

Leadership Core: Character, Competence, and Capacity *Nautilus Book Award for Business and Leadership and Reader Views Reviewers Choice Award*

Hardwiring New Leadership Habits: Does Development Develop? *Readers' Favorite Silver Award and Readers' Favorite Five Stars Award*

The 365 Day Leader: Recalibrate Your Calling Every Day *Midwest Book Awards - Silver Medallion for Business Books and Book Excellence Awards, and the 2026 Distinguished Favorite by the Independent Press Award*

THE OAK STREET TREEHOUSE SERIES by Dick Daniels
The series for early readers that sparks family conversations about faith.

Oak Street Treehouse: The Day They Messaged God (God Made Everything) *Illumination Bronze Book Award and Reader Views Reviewers Choice Award*

Oak Street Treehouse: The Day the New Kid Moved In (God Loves Everybody) *Reader Views Five Star Review and Reader Views Bronze Reviewers Choice Award*

Oak Street Treehouse: The Day They Had a Party (God Is the Host of Heaven) *Illumination Bronze Book Award*

Oak Street Treehouse: The Day They Played Christmas (God Came & Lived Next Door) *Reader Views Five Star Review and the 2026 Distinguished Favorite by the Independent Press Award*

TO MY YOUNG LIFE friends and ministry colleagues serving faithfully throughout Scandinavia. Your sacrificial commitment to building authentic relationships with the delightful Nordic young people reflects the heart of Christ Jesus. With ancestral roots in Norway, Sweden and Denmark, I am deeply grateful for your growing ministry in a culture where faith is often overlooked. Your passion to introduce students to Jesus is both rare and inspiring. I look forward to volunteering on Young Life's Work Crew with you once again at the next high school camp in Norway. Thank you for the privilege of being part of your team that is helping the next generations reconsider Jesus and reconstruct their faith.

I thank my God every time I remember you. In all my prayers for all of you, I always pray with joy. **PHILIPPIANS 1:3-4**

DICK DANIELS

Dishwasher
Table Server
Whatever Is Needed

Table of Contents

PREFACE

MANY OF US REACH a time in life when the Jesus we were introduced to, or observed second hand through the life of other religious people, doesn't seem to match the Jesus we are searching for, hoping to find, or willing to keep following now. Somewhere along the way, questions showed up, and they refused to leave quietly.

You may be looking at the possibility of reading this book each day for an entire year because something in you is still wondering about Jesus, or you are willing to consider if a more honest and credible faith is possible. It can be a genuine hunger for clarity in wrestling with the questions that may not have easy answers.

Maybe the unfairness of life has cracked open your assumptions. Maybe the voices you trusted have disappointed or offended you. Maybe the answers you were handed as a child no longer satisfy the complexity of your adult world. Whatever the reason, you are contemplating taking this next year to wonder, examine, dismantle, reconstruct, or even continue to doubt faith. That can feel wrong or lonely, and it can be filled with some level of anxiety. Perhaps the disconnects of faith with life as you find it are finally emboldening you to seek other answers elsewhere.

Be encouraged. There is a long and sacred history of God's people wrestling their way into a deeper, truer faith. Jacob wrestled with God. David questioned God. Jeremiah lamented it all. Thomas doubted Jesus' resurrection. Paul rebuilt his entire worldview after spending years trying to stop the Jesus movement and faith development for people of his day. Growth often begins with disorientation that leads to asking or trying to answer honest questions.

"Deconstruction" is not the enemy of faith. As a matter of fact, it can be the uncomfortable hallway between spiritual rooms. It's the honesty of saying: *Something here needs to change if I am going to keep following Jesus.* Yet deconstruction is not a destination. If we only tear down our home, we are left with no place to live. The Christian journey invites us to reconstruct our faith—to build and rebuild our beliefs, practices, and identity around the person of Christ, the account of Jesus' life, death, and resurrection included in Scripture, and the transforming work of the Holy Spirit at work within us.

This book is not an invitation to abandon what is true, but to clear away what is brittle. It is a companion for the journey from inherited assumptions to a more resilient, lived-in faith — a faith that can stand up to doubt, disappointment, science, suffering, shifting culture, and the messiness of real life. It's a faith that can lead to a counterintuitive "other-centered" life.

If you are in a season of questioning, you are not alone and you are not a disappointment, even in God's eyes. Maybe a disappointment in your church or your family or your circle of friends, I do not know, but definitely not with God. You may actually be closer to spiritual renewal than you realize. Jesus isn't afraid of your questions. He meets you in them. So many of David's psalms in the Old Testament are emotional expressions of his struggle with understanding or disagreeing with God's ways of working.

Let's take this journey together while we are unafraid to pull apart what needs re-examining and rebuild what is transformative and true. Welcome to the work of faith made new. Now, let's take a deeper dive into the relationship between deconstructing and reconstructing faith.

Deconstructing Faith

Deconstructing your faith is asking, "What do I believe, and why?" It means taking a hard look at the beliefs you grew up with or once held.

» It often begins when someone feels doubt, disappointment, or confusion, or it happens after painful experiences in church or a religious community.

» It can lead to asking questions about long-standing teachings, noticing gaps between what people say and actually do, or letting go of traditions and cultural habits that are unnecessarily coupled with one's faith. Some will conclude their reconsideration by saying, "I'm spiritual but not religious." They don't want to give up on faith, but they are letting go of religious practices that have distracted them from reconsidering Jesus and ultimately from following Jesus.

» Done well, it can help strip away false, questionable practices, or beliefs disconnected from the essential core of following Jesus, at least for now.

» The shadow side of deconstruction is that it can also turn into bitterness, anger, depression, or just walking away from faith completely while losing any connection with God.

2 CORINTHIANS 10:4-5; MATTHEW 23:27-28

Reconstructing Faith

» Reconstructing your faith is asking, "What can I hold onto, and how will I live it out?" It means intentionally rebuilding your spiritual life after pulling apart what doesn't hold up in your reconsideration of Jesus.

» It's about holding onto what is true, life-giving, and solely centered on Jesus—especially the reason for his death and the reality of his resurrection. It leads to personal transformation for those who end up choosing to follow or re-follow Jesus.

» It comes from a longing for something real, a faith strong enough to face doubts, life's challenges, and your own need for intellectual integrity and credibility.

» Done well, it keeps the heart of faith—trust in God—while pausing the self-imposed or other-imposed weight of rigid rules or dysfunctional systems. It results in a deeper, more personal, and more compassionate faith that helps one connect with others who are also wrestling with belief.

EZEKIEL 36:26-27; COLOSSIANS 2:6-7

DECONSTRUCTION WITHOUT RECONSTRUCTION This often leaves someone in a state of suspension—free from old traditions or harmful systems—but without a firm foundation that guides one through life. Without rebuilding, people miss the grounding that comes from the counter-cultural teaching of Jesus. His truths are anchored in eyewitness accounts of lives so transformed that they sparked a movement that is still reshaping every facet of the world today.

RECONSTRUCTION WITHOUT DECONSTRUCTION. This can create a shallow or secondhand faith that crumbles under the weight of issues and challenges of living in a broken world. Blindly adopting someone else's belief system or clinging to empty religious structures adds baggage and risks missing the heart of what it means to follow Jesus.

Both ... in the Right Order

Together, deconstruction and reconstruction can produce a tested, refined, and personal faith—one you truly own. It is rooted in the actual historical events of Jesus that are echoed every week when Christ followers gather for times of worship and application-oriented teaching on every continent and in every culture.

Following Jesus isn't blind faith—it's a reasoned belief in the God who loves the world so much that he sent his Son to show us who God is in character, in mercy, in grace, in justice, in power over evil, and in a love that transcends those who may not be like us or never will like us. Yes, that even includes our enemies!

"For no one can lay any foundation other than the one already laid, which is Jesus Christ."

1 CORINTHIANS 3:11

What it Means for Me

I have three choices: deconstruct, reconstruct, or both, and in that order. If I deconstruct and reconstruct my faith and come to the end of my life only to discover there is nothing beyond the grave—what have I really lost? By following Jesus' radical call to an other-centered life—even to love my enemies—I will have lived by the law of love (see John 13:34-35). That is never a loss! The legacy and reputation I leave behind will honor each coming generation of my family and the workplace culture I positively contributed to.

If I deconstruct my faith without reconstruction and disregard God, leaving any semblance of faith behind, and I face eternity only to discover that God is real and there is more beyond the grave—then I will have lost everything. I will then regret that I turned my back on the God who created me, loved me, died for me, and now lives on without me. Along with my friends, who also walked away, we will never know what could have been in a life of following Jesus

"If anyone is in Christ, the new creation has come:

The old has gone, the new is here!"

— 2 CORINTHIANS 5:17

Reconstructing Faith,
DR. DICK DANIELS

www.the365DayLeader.org
info@theLDG.org

INTRODUCTION

What? So What? Now What?

WHAT IF a clearer picture of Jesus could change everything you thought you knew about faith—and about yourself? I wish I had understood Jesus with greater clarity much sooner in life. Not the Jesus we often filter through religious structures and systems of belief, but the Jesus we are introduced to in the Bible who walked for 33 years where we walk. This is the Jesus who sees us, knows us, understands us, cares about us, and is willing to walk with us guiding us through our entire life experience.

This book offers a year-long first look, or may be a year-long second look, at the person of Jesus Christ. Who is he? Where did he come from? What did he say and do? Why did he say and do those things? What was the result of his life here on earth? What is it about God's story of Jesus that I don't understand yet? And then the tougher question: What difference, if any, does Jesus make in my life?

I am inviting you to spend a few minutes every day for an entire year rediscovering Jesus. Come at this with the honesty of an open mind along with curiosity, grace, and a sense of humor. Notice along the way how hope may awaken where you may least expect it, where faith once felt fractured. Rediscovering Jesus leads to asking and answering three persistent questions: What? So what? Now what?

What are the possible answers to my questions about a faith I have deconstructed, or I think about deconstructing, or perhaps a faith I never engaged with?

So what do I do with the answers provided to my questions from friends and family or the new insights I gain from the record of those who were first century eyewitnesses to the death and resurrection of Jesus?

Now what might it mean for my life, my value system, and my choice of whether or not to follow Jesus?[1]

Join me to reconsider Jesus or to reconstruct faith. I hope to intrigue you through a somewhat linear but very dynamic sequence of Jesus' story from the first page of the Bible to the last. Nine actions describe the adventurous journey of reconstructing faith during these next 365 days. This exercise could literally change your life:

Considering – Moving from deconstructing your faith to reconstructing your faith in Jesus.

Introducing – Discovering a coherent overview of the Bible's account of Jesus.

Exploring – Beginning to see into the lives of ordinary people throughout the New Testament what it means to follow Jesus. These first-century individuals are not that different from you and me in their personalities, interests, life challenges, quirks, and values!

Reminding – For those with a religious background, much of this book will be a refresher. For others, it will be an introductory overview which explains the literature in the Bible, the personalities included, the 66 documents or letters written by 40 people over 1,500 years, on 3 continents, in 3 languages with one central theme throughout.

Understanding – The intent is to move the reader from just gathering more information, to grasping the essence of the Bible's consistent introduction to the God of Heaven and his redemptive work in the creation he loves.

Choosing – The reader has a free-will opportunity to buy-in to Jesus' example, teaching, and invitation or to move on in their own value system needed to make sense of life and the world they live in.

Applying – For those who choose to follow Jesus, the adventure begins by taking incremental steps of growth, followed by personal change and transformation in the way you live with an "other's first" approach, filled with the humility and grace of Jesus.

Living – This isn't about trying to live a perfect life or one without challenges, but it's the experience of the abundant life Jesus promises (see John 10:10). It's living with a sightline to the Sovereign God who is working out his purposes in spite of the choices made by imperfect people living in a broken and fallen world.

Anticipating – Spending eternity in the presence of God with a cloud of witnesses who are thanking God for his mercy and grace demonstrated so prominently in the life, death, and resurrection of Jesus.

Reconstructing Faith: 365 Days to Reconsider Jesus takes a look at nine relevant insights in the Old and New Testaments:

1. Timeline of the Bible including the 400 years of silence between the Old and New Testaments.

2. Old Testament anticipation of the Messiah including specific prophecies of where he will be born, his character, and his ultimate destiny.

3. New Testament record of Jesus' life as a fulfillment of Old Testament prophecy and expectation.

4. Kingdom message of his teaching and mission to make his Heavenly Father known personally while fully accessible to anyone anywhere in the world.

5. Global movement of following Jesus as it began with the first century followers in the city of Jerusalem.

6. Formation of local Jesus' gatherings in the Mediterranean world and eventually to the ends of the earth.

7. End-game of what God's stepping into the human story is all about.

8. God's ultimate victory over all that is evil.

9. Reality of an eternity with or without God.

This writing is not my personal account of Jesus. It's not my religious philosophy. It's not my spin on what the Bible says, and what I think it means. It's simply capturing 365 puzzle pieces that makeup the Bible's record of God's amazing and grace-filled account of restoring a lost and broken world to what he originally intended in the Garden of Eden. Jesus' invitation to follow him is a choice that only you can make. No one can make it for you. In this book, I only want to be sure you have the full unfiltered story of Jesus.

HISTORY IS "HIS-STORY!"

1. This book outlines the "What?"

2. Next ask, "So What?" So, what is its meaning for you: Where did you come from? Who are you? Why are you here? How should you live? What happens after you die? Who or what can you trust?

3. Finally ask, "Now What?" Now what will you do with Jesus? Accept him? Reject him? Commit to learning more? Are you ready to take the next step in reconsidering Jesus?

Following Jesus is not just about a set of beliefs. It is doing something with what you believe. Beliefs are the "What?" of reconstructing faith. Living what you believe in your daily life answers the "So What?" and "Now What?" questions. It is following what Jesus taught and what he modeled in an "other-centered" approach to life. It touches every re-lationship, every decision, and every conversation through your daily choices of the attitudes you hold, the words you use to express those attitudes, and the behaviors that reflect your words. Keep reading, perhaps only a few minutes each day. Keep reconsidering Jesus. Keep reconstructing your faith. Finally, let me know your comments, your questions, and your decisions along the way in this 365 day journey – maybe to take one last look at Jesus.

Rediscovering Jesus,
DR. DICK DANIELS

www.the365DayLeader.org
info@theLDG.org

STAGES OF
RECONSTRUCTING
FAITH

From Disbelief to Transformation: A Developmental Journey of Faith

FAITH IS NOT A STRAIGHT LINE. It can be questioned, dismantled, and rebuilt. It bends, breaks, and deepens as life unfolds. This model is offered as a compassionate framework for understanding that journey. It describes three broad phases people often experience as they reconsider Jesus: **Rejection**, **Reevaluation**, and **Renewal**. These phases are not rigid or linear. People may move forward, step back, skip stages, or revisit earlier questions with new insight. The model does not diagnose or prescribe; it simply names the realities many will encounter as they deconstruct and reconstruct their spiritual lives.

Reconstructing faith is ultimately a story of invitation. Jesus does not fear our questions, avoid our doubts, or dismiss our pain. Instead, he meets us in every phase and gently leads us toward a faith that is more personal, more resilient, and more rooted in who he truly is.

REJECTION OF FAITH — The Certainty of Disbelief
A season marked by skepticism, cynicism, and the unraveling of once-held beliefs.

Disbelief – A settled conviction that there is no God or higher power; reality is explained without reference to the divine (Atheism).

Uncertainty – Unsure if God exists and assumes that ultimate truth about the divine is unknowable (Agnosticism).

REEVALUATION OF FAITH — Asking Hard but Honest Questions
A necessary and often challenging process of reassessing beliefs in light of life experiences, intellectual struggles, and even painful encounters within a faith community that can no longer be ignored.

Questioning – Intellectual, emotional, or personal experiences that provoke honest reconsideration of previously accepted beliefs.

Disillusionment – Deep frustration arising from hypocrisy, moral failure, or inconsistency observed in family members, friends, or religious leaders.

Doubt – Lingering uncertainty about core beliefs or secondary doctrines that lack satisfying, credible answers to sincere questions.

Cynicism – A guarded skepticism toward faith, often fueled by religious abuse, the misuse of power, or the perception that faith requires intellectual compromise when one's questions are dismissed.

Withdrawal – Stepping back from organized religion, spiritual practices, or faith altogether as a means of self-protection in one's search for greater clarity and intellectual reason.

RENEWAL OF FAITH — Learning to Follow Jesus
Rebuilding a faith that is thoughtfully examined, deeply personal in its daily practice, and grounded in the life and teachings of Jesus.

Awakening – A renewed spiritual awareness that is often "spiritual but not religious," marked by longing without rooted connection to a faith community.

Belonging – Reengaging with a Christian community where essential beliefs are clearly taught, safely explored, and faithfully lived.

Alignment – Integrating the teachings of Jesus into daily life through Christlike attitudes, words, and behaviors.

Growth – A deliberate commitment to formative spiritual practices that cultivate obedience, deepen trust, and recalibrate the soul.

Transformation – Ongoing maturity in Christlike character, expressed through faithful stewardship of God-given time, treasure, and talent.

STAGES OF **RECONSTRUCTING** FAITH

From **Disbelief** to **Transformation**: A Developmental Journey of Faith

REJECTION OF FAITH

The Certainty of Disbelief

Disbelief
Uncertainty

REEVALUATION OF FAITH

Asking Hard but Honest Questions

Questioning
Disillusionment
Doubt
Cynicism
Withdrawal

RENEWAL OF FAITH

Learning to Follow Jesus

Awakening
Belonging
Alignment
Growth
Transformation

© TheLDG.org

JANUARY

IN CHRIST ALONE

*"There is salvation in no one else!
God has given no other name under
heaven by which we must be saved."*

— ACTS 4:12

In Christ Alone

In Christ alone my hope is found,
He is my light, my strength, my song;
This Cornerstone, this solid Ground,
Firm through the fiercest drought and storm.
What heights of love, what depths of peace,
When fears are stilled, when strivings cease!

My Comforter, my All in All,
Here in the love of Christ I stand.
In Christ alone! – who took on flesh,
Fullness of God in helpless babe.
This gift of love and righteousness,
Scorned by the ones he came to save:

Till on that cross as Jesus died,
The wrath of God was satisfied –
For every sin on Him was laid;
Here in the death of Christ I live.
There in the ground His body lay,
Light of the world by darkness slain:

Then bursting forth in glorious day
Up from the grave he rose again!
And as he stands in victory
Sin's curse has lost its grip on me,
For I am his and he is mine –
Bought with the precious blood of Christ.

No guilt in life, no fear in death,
This is the power of Christ in me;
From life's first cry to final breath,
Jesus commands my destiny.
No power of hell, no scheme of man,
Can ever pluck me from His hand:
Till he returns or calls me home,
Here in the power of Christ I'll stand.[2]

01

Your Timeline in Following Jesus

New Year's Day is a new beginning. The Apostle Paul says, "I focus on this one thing: Forgetting the past and looking forward to what lies ahead, I press on to reach the end of the race and receive the heavenly prize for which God, through Christ Jesus, is calling us" (Philippians 3:13-14). How can you start this new year? Think in terms of the time frame of your life:

Past – Learn from it, make amends, let it go.

Present – Represent Jesus in every situation, decision, conversation, and relationship.

Future – Live with confidence in God's second chances with optimism of his promise of a better eternal day to come.

ROMANS 15:4

02

Your Talk and Your Walk

Following Jesus is more about behavior than it is about belief. Think of it like this:

- Belief – 49%
- Behavior – 51%

> *"Do not merely listen to the word and so deceive yourselves. Do what it says."*

JAMES 1:22

03

God's Distinctive

God doesn't wait for us to find him and then ask us to die for him to pay the price of our forgiveness. God found us and then died for us to pay the price that was due for our forgiveness. That simple truth makes Christianity uniquely different from every other claim to true religion or deity.

ROMANS 5:8

04

God's Love Made Simple

Mercy – When we ask God to forgive our sin and he with-holds the consequences we really deserve.

Grace – When God blesses us in life by giving us more than we dare ask or imagine and don't deserve.

"The Lord is compassionate and gracious,
slow to anger, abounding in love"

PSALM 103:8-12

05

Happiness or Joy?

Happiness is external. It is an emotion of the moment. It is the result of how you react to what is happening around you. When life is good you are happy.

Joy is internal. It is a deep-seated attitude that you bring into every situation and conversation in life. Joy defies circumstances.

Joy is the result of how you prioritize life:

> **J**esus ... first
>
> **O**thers ... second
>
> **Y**ou ... third

ROMANS 15:13

06

Are You Full of It?

When the Apostle Paul wrote a letter to the followers of Jesus in the city of Ephesus, he knew that people will choose what they fill their mind with. He understood that what influences them affects how they do and see every part of their life. It's true for people today, not just in the first century. In that letter, Paul invites them to be full of the Holy Spirit rather than other influences. His point is this: It's not how much of the Holy Spirit you have but how much of you the Holy Spirit has.

Being full of the Holy Spirit means you are continually making the choice to let God's presence touch every aspect of your life rather than let other things have priority and influence on you down a path leading you away from Jesus. When the Holy Spirit is guiding, empowering, and transforming your character and conduct, it leads you into a continual daily adventure of becoming more like Jesus.

EPHESIANS 5:18-20

07

How to Deconstruct Your Faith

Are you critically examining the beliefs you once held to be true? One guardrail for honest re-evaluation: Don't throw the baby out with the bathwater!

The Bathwater: Religious systems and traditions that are no longer meaningful, or your not-so-positive church experience, or self-righteous Christians who talk but don't walk the truth, or a flippant conclusion that you no longer need a higher power in your life.

The Baby: Jesus

COLOSSIANS 3:1-2

08

How God Works

During our worst experiences, God works *in* us...so in the worst experiences of others he can work *through* us.

> "*Praise be to the God and Father of our Lord Jesus Christ, the Father of compassion and the God of all comfort, who comforts us in all our troubles, so that we can comfort those in any trouble with the comfort we ourselves receive from God.*"

2 CORINTHIANS 1:3-4

09

When Life's Not Easy

Facing and getting through tough times does not go unnoticed by God. He knows. He cares. He is at work.

"Consider it all joy, my brothers and sisters,
whenever you face trials of many kinds,
because you know that the testing
of your faith produces perseverance.
Let perseverance finish its work
so that you may be mature and complete,
not lacking anything."

JAMES 1:2-4

10

Following Jesus' Ethical Example

Followers of Jesus do the right thing to help the most...and harm the least, regardless of the cost.

> *"Love does not harm to a neighbor.*
> *Therefore, love is the fulfillment of the law"*

ROMANS 13:8-10

11

How Right Are You?

Humble .... Self-Righteous

Jesus tells us not to judge others. Why? It is such a holy act that God reserves judgment for himself.

In contrast to our human tendency to pass judgment on others, Jesus calls followers to a higher standard. We are to love others in the same way Jesus demonstrated love for us...even our enemies.

MATTHEW 7:1-3

12

God's Business Plan

Vision – A redeemed community in a heavenly eternity. Revelation 21

Mission – Go, make disciples of all nations, baptize and teach them to obey all I have commanded. Mark 12:30-31

Values – Love God, your neighbor, yourself, and your enemy. Matthew 22:37-39; 5:44

Strategy – Two by two. Mark 6:7

Structure – Local gatherings of Jesus' followers. Acts 2:42-47

Staffing – Everyone who believes and follows Jesus' teaching and example daily. 1 Corinthians 12:27

Systems – The Son died. We build relationships with people far from God. The Father draws people to Jesus. The Holy Spirit convicts people of their sin and teaches people to understand and obey Jesus' teaching.

JOHN 6:44; 16:8-11, 13

13

Is Grace Overrated?

In the Bible, God sees mistakes as sin when we hurt others or hurt ourselves

Followers of Jesus access God's amazing grace to live more like Christ when four things are true:

1. When followers regret mistakes

2. When followers own mistakes

3. When followers make amends for mistakes

4. When followers learn from their mistakes

Maybe grace is never overrated. Maybe the power of sin is underrated!

ROMANS 6:1-2

14

Parenting Boundaries

The wisdom of the Apostle Paul writing to parents in the church in Ephesus says: "Do not provoke your children to anger but bring them up in the discipline and instruction of the Lord" (Ephesians 6:4).

Provoke means continual irritation, harshness, and unpredictability.

> Parenting Question: Do you praise your children for doing the right things and doing things in the right way more than you punish your children for doing the wrong things or especially doing things in the wrong way according to your preferences?

Anger means deep resentment more than momentary frustration.

> Parenting Question: Every emotion has choices in terms of intensity. When a child makes a mistake, where are you on the continuum from being mad to being angry to being out of control? Where does that deep resentment come from when you are angry or especially when you are out of control? What is the root cause of the tendency to over react rather than respond to mistakes with a developmental mindset that invites growth and improvement?

PROVERBS 15:1

15

How to Look Like Jesus

Following Jesus and becoming more like Jesus is not a destination achieved overnight, but a lifelong journey of incremental spiritual growth and change. Spiritual maturity is shaped by God's grace and our active participation. It's an adventure that impacts every aspect of who you are, how you live, and how you relate to people of all shapes and sizes.

Attitudes – How you think

Words – How you talk

Behaviors – How you act

2 PETER 1:5-8

16

Jesus the Christ

For many people, "Jesus Christ" is essentially an exclamation to whatever else they are saying or sometimes a statement of condemnation to another person. Some religiously minded people think of it as Jesus' first and last name.

Jesus is his name. Christ is a title of who he is: Jesus the Christ means Jesus the King.

The third of the Ten Commandments says not to misuse God's name. It is perhaps one of the most challenging of the ten: "You shall not misuse the name of the Lord your God, for the Lord will not hold anyone guiltless who misuses his name."

EXODUS 20:7

17

When Is Bad Too Bad?

The short story is that Jesus died on a cross to forgive sin for all of humankind. The rest of the story is that Jesus rose from the dead, and his resurrection was evidenced by a long list of eyewitnesses.

What Jesus did leads to this question: Is my sin so bad that I don't deserve to be forgiven by anyone? The Apostle Paul asked that question about himself until he understood the significance of Easter. The short story explains how amazing God's grace is for anyone and everyone. The rest of the story tells how sinful but forgiven people can now live a new kind of life under the guidance and power of God's Holy Spirit.

Easter is the day that changed everything forever for everyone everywhere.

1 CORINTHIANS 15:3-10

18

Uncommon Relatives of Jesus

We know the big names: Abraham, Isaac, Jacob, Joseph, David, and Mary.

There are forty-two genealogical generations from Abraham to Jesus. Tamar? Rahab? Ruth? Uriah's Wife? Matthew records these names among the 51 or so in his genealogy of Jesus. There is not a normal family anywhere in the Bible, so you are in good company.

Welcome to the family!

MATTHEW 1:1-17

19

God the Father's Job Description

Creator and Sustainer – Creates and sustains the heavens and earth.

Sovereign Ruler – Reigns as King over all nations and powers.

Father of his People – Provides, disciplines, and guides with care and compassion.

Sender of the Son – Sends Jesus the Christ into the world for salvation.

Giver of the Holy Spirit – Promises and sends the Holy Spirit to empower and guide believers.

Judge and Rewarder – Brings justice to the world and rewards the faithful while holding everyone accountable to his standards.

Eternal Father – Loves and sustains while His character and presence are forever unchanging.

1 CORINTHIANS 8:6

20

When Is the Spirit Holy?

Presence and Power – The Holy Spirit is the breath of God who was also at creation giving life to all that is living.

Revelation and Inspiration – Inspiring prophets and revealing truth.

Guidance and Transformation – Fruit of the Spirit, convicts of sin, and guides people in applying God's wisdom.

Empowerment for Mission – Pentecost is when the Holy Spirit was given to believers. At that time:

>...Spiritual gifts were given to believers to serve the local church.

>...Believers are equipped for specific tasks assigned by God.

>...That work of the Holy Spirit continues today.

Presence in Believers – Dwells within believers, gives assurance of salvation, is the helper and comforter.

JOHN 14:26

21

Jesus' Job Description

The Word Made Flesh – The eternal Word of God who became human. Through him, creation came into being and redemption is made possible.

The Son of God – Fully divine, fully human. Reveals the nature & character of God.

The Messiah & Savior – The promised one whose death would save humanity from sin. His resurrection demonstrated God's power over sin and death.

Teacher & Example – Taught about love, forgiveness, and righteousness in the Kingdom of God while his life modeled humility, obedience, and compassion.

Mediator & High Priest – The mediator who intercedes for believers before God.

Judge & Rewarder – Brings justice to the world & rewards the faithful while holding everyone accountable to his standards.

King & Lord – Jesus the Christ, the King of Kings who inaugurated the Kingdom of God and will return to fully establish it for all eternity.

ROMANS 10:9

22

Who Saw Jesus Dead and Alive?

Jesus died on the cross between two thieves who also died. He was raised from the dead by God the Father. Jesus was seen by hundreds after the resurrection: Mary Magdalene, several other women, Peter, two disciples on the road to Emmaus, eleven of the disciples together, James his earthly brother, and more than 500 people at one place.

Jesus appeared indoors, outdoors, in Jerusalem, Galilee, in homes of people. The resurrection was not a rumor. It was witnessed, verified, and recorded for all history. The appearances proved more than the fact that he was alive. The appearances empowered the movement that became the church and transformed fearful followers into world-changing witnesses of Christ crucified and risen.

1 CORINTHIANS 15:3-8

23

The Shepherd's Psalm

Provision. "The Lord is my shepherd; I shall not want" (Psalm 23:1).

Rest & Renewal. "He makes me to lie down in green pastures. He leads me beside the still waters. He restores my soul" (Psalm 23:2-3).

Guidance. "He leads me in the paths of righteousness for his name's sake" (Psalm 23:3).

Protection. "When I walk through the valley of the shadow of death, I will fear no evil: for you are with me; your rod and your staff comfort me" (Psalm 23:4).

Blessing. "You prepare a table before me in the presence of my enemies. You anoint my head with oil; my cup overflows" (Psalm 23:5).

Hope. "Surely goodness and mercy will follow me all the days of my life; and I will dwell in the house of the Lord forever" (Psalm 23:6).

PSALM 23

24

When Tongues Get You in Trouble

Speaking in tongues – 1 Corinthians 14:19

The tongue is powerful – Proverbs 18:21

The tongue and sin – James 3:5-6

The tongue and lying – Proverbs 120:2

The tongue and gossip – Proverbs 10:18

The tongue and cursing – James 3:9-10

The tongue and spiritual maturity – James 1:26

COLOSSIANS 4:6

25

Questions Jesus Asked

Question #1: About Getting Well

In John's Gospel account of Jesus' ministry, Jesus asks the obvious question of one sick person: "Do you want to be made well?" (John 5:5-6). Healing begins with a desire and willingness to change. Some people have learned to live sick or leverage their sickness to the detriment of others. Healing often requires people to take steps in the direction of being responsible for a new way of living. It starts with wanting change. Jesus worked with people willing to change. If they were not willing to change, then he moved on. Concerned and compassionate, yes, but he moved on to others more receptive to the help he could offer.

When we want to be seen by others as a compassionate Christian, we feel obligated, even guilty, to stay even when another is unwilling to change. We are not responsible to stay in hopes that they will see what they are doing at your expense or the expense of your family, or even at the expense of their own life and health. It's not our responsibility to stay trying to get them to want to change. Don't stay accepting their abuse because you think that is the Christian thing to do. Sometimes not staying is the wakeup call they needed to face the reality of who they have become.

2 CORINTHIANS 12:9

26

The Bible in Two Parts

Part One – The Old Covenant (Testament)

The Old Covenant was God's law given to ancient Israel through Moses, including Torah, commandments, and ceremonial practices.

- It was God's covenant specifically for ancient Israel, shaping its national, religious, and moral life. See: Galatians 3:24.

- It defined the pattern of obedient living by which Israel would experience God's blessing. See: Deuteronomy 6:24.

- It carried God's intention to bless all nations through Israel.

- It was given in anticipation of something greater yet to come, and was never intended to be for the whole world.

- It ultimately found its fulfillment and completion in Jesus and therefore no longer defines how Christians relate to God. See: Hebrews 8:13.

Part Two – The New Covenant (Testament)

The New Covenant was inaugurated through the life, teaching, death, and resurrection of Jesus.

- Its authority rests not in the perfection of the Law, but in the person of Jesus the Christ—God incarnate.

- Its ethical center is love rather than rule-keeping.

- It calls for wholehearted love of God expressed through self-giving love for one's neighbor.

- It continually asks the guiding question: What does Jesus' kind of love require of me here and now?

- It brings the Old Covenant's story of redemption to completion through the once-for-all sacrifice of Jesus for the sins of the world.

Then he said, "Look, I have come to do your will." He cancels the first covenant in order to put the second into effect. For God's will was for us to be made holy by the sacrifice of the body of Jesus Christ, once for all time.

HEBREWS 10:9-10

27

Worry Wart

A 1920s syndicated comic strip called "Out Our Way" by J.R. Williams featured a mischievous little boy called Worry Wart. He never worried, but everyone else around him worried because of him. We use the term today for anyone who worries excessively. Jesus puts it all in perspective when he asks the question: "Which of you by worrying can add a single hour to your life?" (Matthew 6:27).

Worrying is unproductive. No amount of anxiety can change anything. God knows our situation. His promise throughout the Bible reminds us that he will never leave us or forget about us. He goes with us wherever we go and whatever we face. God may not change your situation, but he will change you and see you through any difficulty, so you are still standing on the other side.

MATTHEW 6:27-32

28

Questions Jesus Asked

Question #2: Will I Ever Want What I Already Have?

Jesus asks a piercing question about ultimate priorities: "What good is it to gain the whole world and lose your soul?" (Mark 8:36).

The message is simple. Fame, success, and power mean nothing if you lose your soul. Your soul reflects your relationship with God. It is the eternal part of your being and more valuable than anything temporary. If you spend all your effort chasing what the world offers, it comes at the expense of your relationship with God. In the long run, you keep running further and faster. The antidote? Contentment is the real pathway to work-life balance: Wanting what you already have!

MARK 8:34-38

29

Questions Jesus Asked

Question #3: Who Do You Think Jesus Is?

Jesus' reputation followed him everywhere. Once he asked his group of twelve what others were saying about him. Then Jesus made it personal: "But what about you? Who do you say I am?" (Matthew 16:15).

The question moves any of us from public opinions of Jesus to a deeply personal opinion of Jesus. Who do you think he is? Reconstructing faith isn't about what anyone else thinks about Jesus. It is your own decision and conviction. It's a timeless question.

Each person must wrestle with who Jesus is. creative teacher? popular prophet? Son of God? The evidence of Jesus' death and then his resurrection is the event in human history that reframes the question. Is Jesus who he claimed to be? Who is he to you? What difference does it mean in how you live in light what he taught and how he lived?

MATTHEW 16:13-20

30

In a Boat without a Paddle

Have you ever been on the water in a small boat in a storm? There's nothing more terrifying than water and wind! I know. I live on the Gulf coast of Florida and have endured a few hurricanes in the last ten years. Jesus' group of twelve were in a boat with Jesus when a storm blew in. He was doing a power nap while they were at wit's end of how to deal with a powerful storm. They woke him up. He saw their situation and asked, "Why are you afraid, O you of little faith?" (Matthew 8:26).

In the storms of life, fear is normal. We may be wondering where God is. Maybe he doesn't care? Maybe he can't or won't do anything about your situation? Be reminded that God controls both the storms of nature and the storms of a troubled life. He is there. He does care. He may calm your storm or calm you in the storm.

MATTHEW 8:23-27

31

Three Gods or One?

The one true God exists eternally as Father, as Son, and as Holy Spirit. God is one, in essence, and is revealed in three persons who are each fully God. The Trinity is a human description of the unique relationship of the Father, Son, and Holy Spirit. The book by William P. Young called *The Shack* portrays the Trinity as a loving community of equals (Windblown Media, 2007).

The Father's love for a broken world led to his sending his only Son to build a spiritual bridge to close the gap of sin in our relationship with God. When Jesus returned to heaven, the Holy Spirit was sent to live within us to empower us to follow Jesus' teaching and example.

DEUTERONOMY 6:4; MATTHEW 28:19; 2; MARK 1:10-11; ACTS 1:4-5; CORINTHIANS 13:14

FEBRUARY

NO OTHER KING

"The kingdom of the world has become the kingdom of our Lord and of his Messiah, and he will reign for ever and ever."

— REVELATION 11:15

No Other King

No other King would kneel to wash my feet
Prepare a table for his enemies
Lay down his glory for the least of these
No other King would touch a leper's skin
Open his arms to let the outcast in
Respond with mercy in the face of sin

Jesus, no one is like you
Jesus, no one beside you
Of this I am convinced
No greater love exists
Forever all my hope is in no other King

No other King would stand the mockery
Be led to slaughter and refuse to speak
Take up a cross and choose to die with thieves
Take up a cross and give his life for me

Jesus, no one is like you
Jesus, no one beside you
Of this I am convinced
No greater love exists
Forever all my hope is in no other King[3]

01

Radical Love

Love your enemy and pray for those who persecute you! Are you kidding? Jesus isn't just suggesting passive tolerance but is commanding proactive behavior in bringing the goodwill of even your enemy before God in your prayers of intercession. Hatred perpetuates cycles of getting even, but love brings that unending story to a conclusion. Anyone can love friends.

Followers of Jesus change the rules of society by loving the unlovable. Jesus did it. He did it while hanging on the cross: "Father, forgive them, for they know not what they are doing" (Luke 23:34).

Following Jesus means to seek reconciliation, to always respond with kindness rather than react in justifiable anger, and to *counterintuitively* pray for the best of even your worst enemies.

**MATTHEW 5:43-44;
LUKE 23:34**

02

Theology 101
#1: Sanctification

The word literally means "to make holy." When we choose to follow Jesus, the adventure begins in becoming more like Jesus in our character, in our attitudes, in our words, and in our behavior. It isn't about perfection in this life but continual progress by living in a way that reflects God's holiness. That is sanctification.

It's a lifelong process of spiritual growth when the Holy Spirit shapes our character, our desires, and our actions to be a reflection of Jesus and live as his ambassador in every relationship in our lives at home, at work, and in the community.

When Christ returns, our sanctification of becoming more like Christ in our character and behavior, will be completed as we are finally freed from the power of sin and fully conformed to the image of God through his son, Jesus Christ.

JOHN 17:17; GALATIANS 5:22, 23; 1 JOHN 3:2, JAMES 1:2-4; HEBREWS 10:24-25

03

Theology 101
#2: Redemption

In the ancient world, this word was used when freeing slaves or prisoners of war by paying a ransom. It means to buy back or to set free by paying a price. Redemption is both rescue and restoration. It frees us from sin *while* restoring us in our relationship with God and the purpose he has for us in life.

In our lives, we too easily give into the power of sin. Jesus redeems us from the consequences of sin by his sacrificial death on the cross. Then God's power, demonstrated in Christ's resurrection, strengthens us for holy living to avoid giving in.

When we choose to follow Jesus, his redemption means we are forgiven of sin, adopted into God's family, freed from the power of spiritual slavery, and promised eternal life.

MARK 10:45; EPHESIANS 1:7; COLOSSIANS 1:13-14; 1 PETER 1:18-19; REVELATION 5:9

04

At Your Wits' End

When was your last experience of feeling overwhelmed, exhausted, or unsure about what to do next? Psalm 107 describes various people at their wits' end because of their situation in life. No matter how difficult our life might be, this psalm is a reminder that God knows and cares about how tough life can be.

God's lovingkindness surrounds us in those seasons. Those who have experienced God's work in these difficult moments, have a rich understanding of how loving and how caring God is to meet us every time life throws its worst at us.

If you are in that season, listen to Chris Tomlin's worship song, "Whom Shall I Fear" (sixstepsrecords, 2012). The lyrics include: "The one who reigns forever, he is a friend of mine. The God of angel armies is always by my side. And nothing formed against me shall stand. You hold the whole world in your hands. I am holding on to your promises. You are faithful."

When God steps in, it is the end of your wit's end days! God is always more than enough...

**PSALM 107:27; PSALM 34:18; PSALM 46:1;
ISAIAH 43:2; PHILIPPIANS 4:6-7**

05

The Nitwit, Dimwit, and Half-Wit

...**Nitwit** is milder and almost teasing in its tone, meaning foolish or unintelligent.

...**Dimwit** is unflattering and rather blunt, suggesting someone is slow to understand.

...**Half-Wit** is harsh and more offensive in describing someone with very limited mental capacity.

The book of Proverbs in the Old Testament is part of a collection of "wisdom" literature in one section of the Old Testament. In the early chapters of introducing the topic of wisdom, Solomon contrasts the wise with the foolish. At some points, the foolish appear as nitwits. In other verses, the foolish appear as dimwits, and once in a while, the foolish appear to be half-wits! Proverbs 1:7 says, "The fear of the Lord is the beginning of wisdom; fools despise wisdom and instruction."

**PROVERBS 18:2; 12:16; 29:11;
12:15; 26:11; 15:2; 17:28**

06

What Publishing House Did the Bible Come From?

The Bible is one story told through 66 books written by 40 authors over 1500 years! Late in the fourth century, the church established the collection of writings to be included in the Old and New Testaments according to strict criteria for selection and inclusion.

The Old Testament includes a variety of types of literature among its 39 books:
- The Law (5 books), History (12 books), Wisdom and Poetry (5 books), Minor Prophets (12 books), and Major Prophets (5 books).

The New Testament also represents a variety of types of literature among its 27 books:
- Gospels (4 books), History (1 book), Letters (21 books), Prophecy (1 book)

The Bible shows how God works in the lives of imperfect people just like us. Read it. Discuss it. Apply it. Model it. Timothy reminds us of its value: "All Scripture is breathed out by God and profitable for teaching, for reproof, for correction, and for training in righteousness, that the person of God may be complete, equipped for every good work"

2 TIMOTHY 3:16-17

07

Can Women in the Church Lead? Preach?

It all depends on where your theology begins. If you start in Genesis 3 to understand God's thinking, then the consequence of sin affects the role of women as well as the relationship between men and women. If your understanding of God's heart and mind begins in Genesis 1 and 2, then you may come to a different understanding.

God uses the Hebrew word "Ezer" to describe the creation of the woman. Translations often use the word "helper" that suggests Eve was to be the secondary support to Adam. In the context of the Old Testament, "Ezer" is not a term of subordination or weakness. It signifies a powerful equal and vital ally. The woman was to be the equal co-laborer in managing all of creation as God had requested. The term is used twenty-one times in the Old Testament and sixteen of those times, it is used to describe God's strength as the ultimate helper and protector for his people.

Yes, in Genesis 3, sin messed up this relationship throughout the Old Testament, but then Jesus enters God's story in the New Testament fulfilling the old agreement with God while announcing a new and better way of relating to God. Jesus' teaching of the Kingdom of God announced a restoration of all God had originally intended in creation.

We won't get it totally right this side of heaven, but maybe it's time that church leadership gets shared equally with the kind of "helper" God originally intended. The Apostle Paul's letters intended to help churches understand the implications and applications of Jesus' teaching. On this topic he writes, "There is neither Jew nor Greek, slave nor free, male not female, for you are all one in Christ Jesus." God is restoring women to their place of equality as a co-laborer in leading his mission and proclaiming his message, Galatians 3:28.

GENESIS 1:27-28; 2:10-20; JOEL 2:28; ACTS 2:17

08

What Is it About Jesus?

Consider this summary of God's story of Jesus recorded throughout the Bible:

Fully God and fully human. The eternal Son took on human flesh to show us God firsthand.

Conceived by the Holy Spirit. Born of a virgin named Mary.

Sinless life. He lived in perfect obedience to God his heavenly Father.

Crucified. He died on a cross as payment for humanity's sins.

Resurrected. He rose from the grave as God's victory of the ultimate enemy of death.

Ascended. He returned to heaven to sit at the right hand of God the Father.

Coming Again. He will return to be the final judge and to fully establish God's eternal Kingdom.

JOHN 3:16

09

I Thought I Was Pretty Good.
What Happened?

We were created in the image of God with dignity and purpose. Our selfish choices of sin separate us from God. Being good is never good enough to restore our relationship with God. All of humanity needs a Savior and a King to offer us forgiveness and lead us in holy living!

- Have you?
- Want to?
- Will you?
- When?

GENESIS 1:26-27; ISAIAH 59:2;
ROMANS 6:23

10

Do I Have to Go to Church?

It is estimated that somewhere between 8 to 16 million churches exist worldwide. The word for church used in the Bible is *ekklesia*. It does not refer to a building or to an organization. It describes the gathered community of followers of Jesus. It is a global collection of "Jesus' gatherings" that meet regularly for these five main reasons:

1. **To Worship God.** Churches gather to praise, pray, and celebrate God's presence.

2. **For Teaching and Discipleship.** The church is called to make disciples of all nations, teaching people to obey Jesus' wisdom about life in God's Kingdom.

3. **For Community and Fellowship.** Followers of Jesus are called to love one another, support each other, and live as the family of God.

4. **For Service and Mission.** The church is to care for the poor, widows, orphans, and marginalized.

5. **For Telling the Good News.** The church is a witness of Christ by proclaiming the Gospel locally and globally.

EPHESIANS 3:21; MATTHEW 28:19-20; ACTS 2:42-47; JAMES 1:27, ACTS 6:1-7, ACTS 1:8

11

The End

The Bible is focused on how we should live regardless of when Christ's second coming occurs. Jesus said it this way: "But about that day or hour no one knows, not even the angels in heaven, nor the Son, but only the Father" (Matthew 24:36).

What do we know? Four truths summarize the clearest information that we have in the Bible:

1. **The Second Coming** - When Christ returns visibly, bodily, and gloriously

2. **Resurrection of the Dead** – Followers of Jesus are raised to eternal life and surrounded by a cloud of witnesses who together will enjoy a place without sin, tears, mourning, or pain.

3. **The Final Judgment** – God's righteous judgment over all humanity based on one's faith in Christ as demonstrated in their life. Those who choose not to follow Jesus are raised for judgment and the hopeless finality of a painful separation from God and the loss of true community.

4. **New Heavens and New Earth** – God renews creation, removes sin, suffering, and death. Then God commences His eternal dwelling with His people.

**MATTHEW 24:36; 1 THESSALONIANS 4:16;
1 CORINTHIANS 15; JOHN 5:28-29;
REVELATION 20:11-15; MATTHEW 25:31-46.**

12

Seven Things God Hates

1. Haughty eyes.
2. A lying tongue.
3. Hands that shed innocent blood.
4. A heart that devises wicked schemes.
5. Feet that are quick to rush into evil.
6. A false witness who pours out lies.
7. A person who stirs up conflict in the community.

PROVERBS 6: 16-19

13

Life Verses #1 –
What Are You Bragging About?

"Let not the wise boast of their wisdom
or the strong boast of their power
or the rich boast of their wealth,
but let the one who boasts boast about this:
that they have the understanding to know me,
that I am the Lord, who exercises kindness,
justice and righteousness on earth,
for in these I delight declares the Lord."

JEREMIAH 9:23-24

14

Valentine's Day

This is the holiday named after Saint Valentine. He was a Christian martyr from the third century who was executed for his faith and later honored as a saint. Legend says he was a Roman priest who secretly married couples when marriage was banned by Emperor Claudis II. This day became associated with love in the Middle Ages, particularly through the writings of Geoffrey Chaucer, who linked the day to romantic affection and love.

Love is a central theme from the first page of the Bible to the last. The story of Jesus is God's love story for a lost world. Jesus challenges his followers at the Last Supper to a higher quality of love in all relationships. It applies to every conversation, every decision, and action in one's behavior! Do a "love reality check" by reviewing 1 Corinthians 13:4-7. Jesus kept it simple: "Love one another. As I have loved you, so you must love one another."

JOHN 13:34-35

15

A Word Picture of Following Jesus

"Therefore, as you received Christ Jesus the Lord, so walk in him, rooted and built up in him and established in the faith, just as you were taught, abounding in thanksgiving." (Colossians 2:6-7)

...Receiving Christ: Following Jesus begins by receiving Jesus as Savior and Lord.

...Walking in Faith: The life of a Christ follower is not just about starting well but continuing throughout one's lifetime in fellowship and obedience.

...Rooted: Trees that sustain storms are deeply rooted. Faith that continues in a broken and fallen world is grounded in the declaration by eyewitnesses of the only God who died for the sins of the whole world and was resurrected by God the Father to eternal life.

...Built up: Growth never stops. It is lifelong learning and lifelong applying to strengthen habits of living with and relating to people who might not be anything like you.

...Established in the faith: Godly character is the result of living out God's truth in everyday life.

...Thanksgiving: Gratitude in both the overflow of a heart grounded in Christ and God's safeguard for us against discontentment.

COLOSSIANS 2:6-7

16

What Will Heaven Be Like?

One of the most encouraging descriptions of heaven was captured in John's vision in the book of Revelation: "He will wipe away every tear from their eyes, and death will be no more, neither will there mourning, nor crying, nor pain anymore, for the former things have passed away" (Revelation 21:4). With God's gracious presence in heaven, he will wipe away tears showing his tender care and final comfort for those who have suffered during their lifetime.

In heaven the brokenness of our world ends. Sorrow, grief, and the pain of loss that describe life in a broken and fallen world are removed in the age to come. Isaiah 25:8 says, "He will swallow up death forever."

In John's vision in Revelation, God renews everything. The curse is over. Separation from God will never happen again. Suffering will not touch anyone in God's new created order.

REVELATION 21:4;
1 CORINTHIANS 15:54-55

17

Fight the Good Fight

The Apostle Paul steps in between those moments of interpersonal disagreement in writing a letter to the church in Ephesus: "Don't let the sun go down on your anger." (Ephesians 4:26). In other words, settle your arguments before turning out the lights and going to bed.

James, the earthly brother of Jesus, wrote a letter adding to Paul's comments. He offers a way to keep things from getting out of hand. "Everyone should be quick to listen, slow to speak, and slow to become angry" (James 1:19).

In other words, prioritize understanding the other person before saying a word to them.

**EPHESIANS 4:26;
JAMES 1:19**

18

When Bad Is Good for You

Join the Apostle in saying, "We rejoice in our sufferings, knowing that suffering produces endurance, and endurance produces character, and character produces hope." (Romans 5:3-4)

...Trials in your life test your faith by revealing what a broken and fallen world does to people.

...Endurance is built when we continue trusting God under pressure. God is more likely to see you through the challenge than to remove the challenge.

...Character is the refined result – a faith that is tested is strengthened.

...Our hope is rooted in God's faithfulness not our current circumstances.

**ROMANS 5:3-4;
JAMES 1:2-4**

19

The Fruit Doesn't Fall Far from the Tree – Part One

Yes, children tend to resemble their parents. Our spiritual roots come from our Heavenly Father. Jeremiah echoes this truth: "Blessed is the one who trusts in the Lord, whose confidence is in him. They will be like a tree planted by the water that sends out its roots by the stream. It does not fear when heat comes; its leaves are always green. It has no worries in a year of drought and never fails to bear fruit" (Jeremiah 17:7-8).

Jeremiah's imagery reflects three pairs of words: Dependence and Sustenance, Stability and Security, Growth and Fruitfulness. The fourth pair of words is fear and worry. When your roots are grounded in Christ, the power of fear and worry succumb to his greater power.

**JEREMIAH 17:7-8;
PSALM 1:3**

20

The Fruit Doesn't Fall Far from the Tree – Part Two

Jesus promised his followers that even though he was returning to heaven, he would send another in his place…literally another of the same kind. Jesus was referring to the Spirit of Truth. The Greek word used is generally translated as comforter, advocate, counselor, or helper.

The difference is that Jesus was with them physically and temporarily, but the Holy Spirit would dwell within them spiritually and permanently. As a result, Jesus' followers would not lose his presence, but they would experience it more intimately.

What happens when we accept Paul's words to be filled with the Spirit? Paul says the Spirit produces fruit in us, and these are the results: Love, joy, peace, patience, kindness, goodness, faithfulness, gentleness, and self-control. In which of those nine qualities, do you need the Spirit's help the most?

**JOHN 14:16-17; EPHESIANS 5:18;
GALATIANS 5:22-23**

21

A Cloud of Witnesses

"We are surrounded by such a great cloud of witnesses" (Hebrews 12:1). Hebrews 11 provides an exemplary list of who is included in that cloud. Each story is filled with the challenges of remaining faithful in the face of life at its best and worst. This community of faithful believers from the past testify to God's promises and amazing grace. Their example encourages followers today to continue living in Christlike resilience by keeping their eyes fixed on Jesus.

The Greek word "martys" is translated as "witness" meaning some-one who testifies to God's truth by their words and actions. The lives of these faithful witnesses are a reminder that following Jesus is not a spectator sport!

Picture a marathon race today and the crowd at the finish line cheering every runner who makes it to the end. Their presence inspires endurance, courage, and the pain it may have taken to get there. Entering heaven will be just like that finish line, and the cloud of witnesses will be there when you arrive.

**HEBREWS 11:1-40;
HEBREWS 12:1-3**

22

The Heart of God

*"For God so loved the world so much that he gave his only Son,
so that everyone who believes in him may not die but have eternal life.
For God did not send his Son into the world to be its judge,
but to be its savior."*

JOHN 3:16-17

23

The Virtuous Woman

Proverbs 31:10-31 is like an acrostic poem. The verses begin with the successive letters of the Hebrew alphabet. The poem ends with these words in Proverbs 31:30 describing the virtuous woman: "Charm is deceptive, and beauty does not last, but a woman who fears the Lord will be greatly praised." Why is she praised? Because she personifies these qualities of grace and diligence:

Trustworthy and Diligent: She manages her household with wisdom and care.

Industrious and Resourceful: She engages in trade, business, and provides food and clothing.

Compassionate: She opens her hands to the poor and needy.

Strong and Wise: She is clothed with strength and dignity. She speaks with wisdom and kindness.

Honored: Her children call her blessed, and her husband praises her.

In whom do you see these qualities of character: your grandmother, mother, sister, wife, daughter, friend, co-worker? When did you last praise them for one positive characteristic that you see in them that you wish you had more of?

PROVERBS 31

24

Ten Words to Summarize the Old Testament

1. **Beginnings** – Genesis 1-11, Includes: Adam, Eve, and Noah

2. **Moving** – Genesis 12-50, Includes: Abraham, Isaac, Jacob, and Joseph

3. **Leaving** – Exodus, Includes Moses

4. **Wandering** – Leviticus, Numbers, Deuteronomy, Includes: Moses

5. **Conquering** – Joshua, Includes: Joshua, Rahab, and Caleb

6. **Settling** – Judges, Includes: Deborah, Gideon, and Samson

7. **Uniting** – 1 & 2 Samuel, 1 Kings 1-11, 1 Chronicles, Includes: Saul, David, and Solomon

8. **Dividing** – 1 Kings 1-22, 2 Chronicles, Includes: Rehoboam, Jeroboam, Elijah, Elisha, Isaiah, and Jeremiah

9. **Leaving** – Ezekiel, Daniel, Lamentations, Includes: Nebuchadnezzar, Daniel, and Esther

10. **Returning** – Ezra, Nehemiah, Includes: Ezra and Nehemiah

ROMANS 15:4

25

Salvation Made Simple
Not Simplistic

Grace: It is by grace through faith in Jesus Christ not by our good works that we are saved.

Atonement: Christ's death on the cross paid the ransom due to close the relationship gap between a holy God and a sinful world.

Forgiveness: God's gracious act of pardoning sin and releasing people from guilt and penalty.

Reconciliation: Restoring people into a right relationship with God through Christ.

Eternal Life: A new heaven and a new earth become the community of the faithful where God is the Host of Heaven.

EPHESIANS 2:8-9

26

Forgiveness Is Not Far Fetched

Far-fetched is an adjective that means something is unlikely, improbable, or hard to believe – often because it stretches logic or reality too much. When we live far from God, salvation seems far-fetched. But God came near even though we had moved away. Forgiveness:

It's an act of grace. It's a gift of God's mercy and love.

It's canceling the debt. God cancels the moral debt we owe him due to our sin.

It's removing the guilt. It washes away the weight of our guilt and shame in the face of a holy God.

It's restoring our relationship with God. Our fellowship is restored.

It's guaranteed by the work of Christ. It was his life, death, and resurrection that paid what was due.

**1 JOHN 1:9;
COLOSSIANS 2:13-14**

27

Don't Wait for Hospice

God knows the significance of the relationship between children and their parents. The fifth of the Ten Commandments invites us to honor our parents, and it comes with a promise: "So that you may live long in the land the Lord your God is giving you."

Family respect and obedience is the foundation for a healthy society and long life. How often is it said, "I wish I had said something before they died." The world of hospice suggests a helpful outline for those end-of-life conversations:

Say, **"I love you."**

Say, **"Thank you."**

Say, **"I'm sorry."**

Say, **"Goodbye."**

P.S. No family is perfect! There are no exemplary families to be found in the Bible, but we are still called to honor those who gave us the opportunity at life. Say as many of the four hospice words as you can to those you love and who love you before it is too late.

EXODUS 20:12

28

Theology 101 #3 – The Work of Christ

Incarnation – God becoming human in Jesus Christ.

Atonement – Christ's sacrificial work to reconcile people to God.

Redemption – The act of being bought back from sin's slavery.

Justification – Being declared righteous before God.

Propitiation – Christ's sacrifice satisfying God's justice.

Expiation – The removal of sin and guilt.

HEBREWS 10:12

29

Is it a Leap of Faith to Follow Jesus?

If you are on track in your reading following the calendar, then this is a leap year reading! Most every spiritual journey has a chapter when standing still is no longer an option. Jesus calls us to follow, and his call invites a response. The leap of faith is that moment when we choose to follow Jesus and trust him fully, even when the next step is unclear among our remaining questions about faith.

Following Jesus is always a leap of faith but not blind faith. It is never a leap into unknown darkness. It follows centuries of faithful followers who have asked the tougher questions and concluded that the evidence of the eyewitnesses of Jesus' resurrection and their changed lives grounds their decision in faith.

Spiritual belief is essentially a question about Jesus. Is he who he claimed to be? Either he lied, he was delusional, or he is God who came to live among us. Is it time to take the next step in your faith journey? The next step might be your openness to explore unanswered questions while considering if credible answers exist.

The book of Hebrews defines faith as both trust and confidence. Chapter 11 includes the heroes of faith-filled living. Faith is believing in God's promises before they are fully visible. Faith is not wishful thinking, but a firm conviction rooted in the reliability of God himself.

"Now faith is the substance of things hoped for, the evidence of things not seen."

HEBREWS 11:1

MARCH

HOLY
FOREVER

"Holy, holy, holy is the Lord God Almighty, who was, and is, and is to come."

— REVELATION 4:8

Holy Forever

A thousand generations falling down in worship
To sing the song of ages to the Lamb
And all who've gone before us, and all who will believe
Will sing the song of ages to the Lamb

If you've been forgiven, if you've been redeemed
Sing the song forever to the Lamb
If you walk in freedom, if you bear His name
Sing the song forever to the Lamb

Your name is the highest
Your name is the greatest
Your name stands above them all
All thrones and dominions
All powers and positions
Your name stands above them all

And the angels cry, Holy
All creations cries, Holy
You are lifted high, Holy
Holy forever

Hear your people sing, Holy
To the King of kings, Holy
You will always be, Holy
Holy forever

You will always be, Holy
Holy forever[4]

01

What Does It Mean to be Righteous?

Righteousness refers to someone who is in a right relationship with God and with other people.

- Righteousness is being in a right standing before God
- Righteousness is living in a right relationship with people

The Prophet Micah says it best in three actions. We demonstrate a right relationship with God when we live out these commitments, and we are champions of justice and mercy in our relationships with people when we approach life in these three ways:

1. **Acting justly** – Live with integrity and fairness in all you do.
2. **Loving mercy** – Show compassion and forgiveness to others.
3. **Walking humbly** – Have an attitude of humility and dependence on God.

How righteous are you? Which of Micah's three areas needs attention in your life?

**2 CORINTHIANS 5:21;
MICAH 6:8**

02

Pay It Forward

God never wastes our tough times in life. He is the "grand recycler." The Apostle Paul paints the picture in his second letter to the church in the city of Corinth: "Praise be to the God and Father of our Lord Jesus Christ, the Father of compassion and the God of all comfort, who comforts us in all our troubles..." (2 Corinthians 1:3).

Paul doesn't stop there. He adds a "pay it forward" assignment connected to the tough times of others: "...*so that* we can comfort those in any trouble with the comfort we ourselves receive from God" (2 Corinthians 1:4).

Step One – Be comforted by God in your times of trouble.

Step Two – Comfort others in their times of trouble.

2 CORINTHIANS 1:3-4

03

Outside Looking In

Looking In: People who are not yet following Jesus, are always looking in at those of us who do follow. What are they seeing. Do we inspire them to also follow, or do we give them another reason to keep Jesus at arm's length? See Acts 15:19.

What would it take for you to make following Jesus something your neighbor might be interested in? For that to happen, you need to spend less time in Christian activities and more time where non-followers of Jesus spend their time. God draws people to himself though our relationships where we have earned the right to be heard. Just be a friend who follows Jesus rather than a Jesus' follower with an agenda.

Let them see rather than hear about Jesus. Let them ask when they hit a bump in the road in their own life. Once they ask, then have your Jesus' elevator speech ready. Not long. Just something that intrigues someone wanting more. Carl Medearis' book, *Speaking of Jesus*, offers insight into his mistakes and lessons of how to capture those moments knowing what you might say.

2 CORINTHIANS 6:3

04

Inside Looking Out

Some followers of Jesus become disillusioned. See the example of those who actually knew him in person in John 6:60, 66. Once disillusioned, people contemplate stepping away from a community of faith. It can be the result of life abuse, church abuse, or an intellectual crisis of faith. It leaves people wondering about faith and about God.

What if you just kept your eyes on Jesus? He is described as the Author and Finisher of our Faith in Hebrews. He is the perfect example of what his Heavenly Father is like. It was the reason Jesus left heaven and came to earth: To make his Heavenly Father known and understood.

Every follower of Jesus is an imperfect example of who God is. Maybe it is unfair to expect people like yourself to be as perfect as Jesus. Before you shut the door of the church behind you, to never return again, perhaps accept being part of an imperfect community of people still learning what it means to be more like the perfect Jesus. Just look at Jesus to reconsider your conclusions about God and about faith. Jesus plus nothing. Not Jesus filtered through the life of another imperfect person like yourself. Just Jesus.

HEBREWS 12:2

05

Sometimes a Song Says it Best

I Believe You

*I'd be lying if I said that I'm okay
'Cause right now, I'm lost
And lost count of the broken
prayers I've prayed
And it's true that some days
It'd be easier to doubt
But your word has never let
me down*

*I'll trust You're working even
when my eyes can't see
I won't fear the future 'cause I
know your plans are good for me
And it's true that some days
It'd be easier to doubt
But your word has never let
me down*

*Your love is the reason I hope
Your arms have never let me go
No fear when you know what
I know
Oh Jesus, that's why*

*Your love is the reason I hope
Your arms have never let me go
No fear when you know what
I know
Oh Jesus, that's why*

*I believe you
When you say you're fighting
for me
I believe you
When you tell me that my story
Isn't over just yet
I will rise up again
You promised me that I will make
it through
And I believe you
I believe you[5]*

HABAKKUK 3:17-18

06

The Day Job Lost It All

Friends are important when your dreams disappear. The Old Testament story of Job is the story of friendship.

Eliphaz – Emphasizes that Job's suffering is the result of sin.

Zophar – Asserts that Job deserves worse suffering and calls Job arrogant.

Elihu – Suggests that suffering may serve a disciplinary or instructive role. It's God's tool for growth not retribution.

They all did something right. They came and sat with Job in his grief for seven days and nights and sat in silence.

They all did something wrong. They felt as if they needed to say something that would explain Job's crisis.

Sometimes the best gift of friendship is your presence without trying to explain or justify the pain. Sitting with a friend or family member can be more powerful than ever saying a single word. Your ministry of "presence" to another does not need a script. In God's response to Job, we learn that suffering is not always explained for our understanding or satisfaction on this side of eternity. Trust, humility, and reverence are the best responses as we live this life with the confident hope in a day to come that will be our eternity without tragedy, pain, and suffering.

JOB 42:10-17

07

Faith Is Difficult

Faith is not the absence of doubt. Faith is moving toward God *in spite of doubt*. Faith isn't hard because you're weak. Faith is hard because it is transformational.

Difficult Faith #1 – It Requires Trust Without Full Control. Faith asks us to trust God when: (1) We don't see the full picture, (2) We don't get immediate answers, and (3) We can't control the outcome.

Difficult Faith #2 – It Often Grows in the Dark, Not in the Light. Faith is easy when life is good. Faith becomes real when life if painful.

Difficult Faith #3 – It Requires Letting Go of Self-Reliance. Faith means depending on God more than ourself. That goes against: Our pride, our independence, and our desire to "fix it ourselves.

Difficult Faith #4 – It Requires Choosing God Even When You Don't Understand Him. God is good when life is not. God is working when nothing is happening. God is present when he feels silent. God is faithful when we are not.

"We walk by faith, not by sight."

2 CORINTHIANS 5:7

08

No One Ever Told Me
I Was Gifted

Every follower of Jesus has special abilities or spiritual gifts given by the Holy Spirit for the purpose of building up the church and serving others. These are not natural abilities but God-given empowerments for ministry and encouragement within the body of Christ.

- **Speaking Gifts** – teaching, preaching, prophecy, evangelism, and encouragement
- **Serving Gifts** – helping, leadership, administration, giving, mercy, and hospitality.
- **Sign/Power Gifts** – healing, miracles, tongues, interpretation of tongues, and discernment.

Gifts are given to glorify God, strengthen the church, bring unity and maturity among Jesus followers, and witness to the world of God's power and love.

**1 CORINTHIANS 12; ROMANS 12:6-8;
EPHESIANS 4:11-13; 1 PETER 4:10**

09

I'm Just Following Jesus' Example in Baptism

Jesus' baptism was an example for every follower. What does it represent?

1. Baptism is a symbol of cleansing or the washing away of sin and a new beginning in Christ.

2. Baptism symbolizes an identification with Christ's death and being raised into new life.

3. Baptism is a public declaration of one's faith in Christ and commitment to follow him.

4. Baptism tells the story of one's spiritual adoption as entry into the community of believers of all time, past, present, and future.

**MATTHEW 3:13-17;
ROMANS 6:3-4**

10

The Last Supper Introduced the Lord's Supper

Communion is a time for Christians to remember and celebrate the sacrificial death and resurrection of Jesus: "And he took bread, gave thanks and broke it, and gave it to them, saying, 'This is my body given for you; do this in remembrance of me'" (Luke 22:19).

...It's a proclamation of God's payment for our sin.

...It's a participation that unites believers with Christ and one another.

...It's anticipation of a future heavenly banquet with Christ when he returns.

...The bread represents Christ's body, broken for anyone.

...The cup represents Christ's blood shed for everyone.

It's personal. It's a time of reflection, confession, and gratitude for Christ's sacrifice.

It's interpersonal. It's a demonstration of unity within the body of Christ.

**MARK 14:22-25;
1 CORINTHIANS 11:26**

11

Divisive Church Members

God hates: "one who sows discord among the brothers" (Proverbs 6:16-19). The history of the modern church is littered with stories of churches and pastors destroyed by the selfish voice of a toxic member. Satan does his best work of destroying the church from the inside out.

Divisive church members use their attitudes, words, and actions to create conflict, disunity, or factions within the body of Christ. Their use of divisive gossip, personal slander, or manufactured suspicion pushes their personal agenda at the expense of church unity and community impact.

When these toxic members refuse correction from the wisdom of seasoned and mature church members or from the denominational structures, they become the focus of the teaching in Titus 3:10-11. Paul is writing to his coworker Titus who was leading the church on the island of Crete. He says that repeated refusal by these individuals to repent may require the separation of these people for the health and reputation of the church.

**MATTHEW 18:15-17;
ROMANS 16:17-18**

12

Church Boards and Church Structure

Paul gives insight into church structure and organization when he is writing to Titus: "The reason I left you in Crete was that you might put in order what was left unfinished and appoint elders in every town, as I directed you..." (Titus 1:5). The church structure and organization was unfolding and developing in the early days of the church. Today churches are far more complex in this area. Paul would probably say that clear organization and leadership today is still critical to sustain church ministry and integrity.

- Boards are responsible to ensure alignment with the biblical vision, mission, values, and sound principles of finance. They set broad policies and boundaries for the church's ministry.

- Pastoral staff focus on the operational side of initiating and leading ministry programs that accomplishes the vision and mission.

It can get messy in the middle when boards or board members step out of their policy responsibility and step into managing the strategic operations of the church's day-to-day ministry.

Denominations could best serve their local congregations by continual training of board members who tend to rotate in and out on a periodic basis. Then, have skilled facilitators ready to manage the conflict that too often sidetracks good churches and talented pastors.

TITUS 1:5-9

13

The First Word in the Bible – The Beginning of Creation

The opening verse of the Bible announces God as Creator: "In the beginning God created the heavens and the earth" (Genesis 1:1).

God is the starting point of everything. Life, creation, and history all began in God's hands.

> *"The heavens declare the glory of God;*
> *the skies proclaim the work of his hands.*
> *Day after day they pour forth speech;*
> *night after night they reveal knowledge."*

PSALM 19:1-2

14

The Last Word in the Bible - The Completion of Redemption

In Revelation 22:21, John ends his vision of all that is ahead in God's work with these words: "The Grace of the Lord Jesus be with God's people. Amen."

The last book in the Bible ends by reminding us of grace – the undeserved favor of God given to every follower of Jesus. Grace is a blessing and a benediction to the entire Bible, leaving readers with a reminder of redemption's completion grounded in God's amazing grace to an undeserving humanity.

REVELATION 22:20

15

How Many Years Are Represented in the Biblical Account?

- From Abraham to the end of the Old Testament: 2000 B.C. to 400 B.C. – Approximately 1600 years.

- From the end of the Old Testament to the beginning of the New Testament: 400 B.C. to Zero A.D. – Approximately 400 years.

- From the birth of Jesus to the end of the New Testament record: Zero A.D. to 95 A.D. – Approximately 95 years.

Exact dates and times are widely debated but this provides a rough time frame of the biblical record. Isaiah describes this flow of history this way: "Remember the former things, those of long ago; I am God, and there is no other; I am God, and there is none like me. I make known the end from the beginning, from ancient times, what is still to come."

ISAIAH 46:9-10

16

Creation Points People to God

In the book of Romans, the Apostle Paul reminds those who live far from God that God's existence is not hidden. Paul says it this way: "For since the creation of the world God's invisible qualities – his eternal power and divine nature – have been clearly seen, being understood from what has been made, so that people are without excuse" (Romans 1:20).

Three realities are evident:

1. Creation reveals God's power.

2. Everyone has access to this truth.

3. No one can claim complete ignorance of the God who stands above it all.

The French mathematician, physicist, and Christian thinker, Blaise Pascal (1623-1662), is attributed with saying: "There is a God-shaped vacuum in the heart of each man which cannot be satisfied by any created thing but only by God the Creator, made and known through Jesus Christ."

...God's general revelation in creation reveals who God is (Psalm 19:1-6).

...God's special revelation in Scripture puts words to what we see (Psalm 19:7-14).

...Both testify to the existence and work of the God in heaven.

PSALM 19;
ROMANS 1:18-20

17

How to Love in Real Time

"Love is patient

Love is kind

It does not envy

It does not boast

It is not proud

It does not dishonor others

It is not self-seeking

It is not easily angered

It keeps no record of wrongs

Love does not delight in evil

But rejoices with the truth

It always protects

Always trusts

Always hopes

Always perseveres"

1 CORINTHIANS 13:4-7

18

Questions Jesus Asked

Question #4: Am I judgmental?

"Why do you look at the speck in your brother's (or sister's) eye and pay no attention to the log in your own eye?" (Matthew 7:3). In the Sermon on the Mount, Jesus has just talked about judging others (Matthew 7:1-2). It' all about our tendency to self-righteous hypocrisy. In Matthew's account, Jesus suggests two guardrails for all relationships:

1. Self-examination before judgment.

2. Humility in relationships.

Consider your own shortcomings before pointing out someone else's!

MATTHEW 7:1-5

19

Metaphors for Sin

The Bible often uses descriptive word pictures to help people understand the seriousness of sin and its impact, even for those who profess to follow Jesus. Followers no longer live in sin but still sin while living in a world full of temptations.

Stain – Isaiah 1:18

Debt – Matthew 6:12

Burden – Psalm 38:4

Slavery/Chains – John 8:34

Sickness/Disease – Mark 2:17

Darkness – John 3:19

Missing the Mark – Romans 3:23

Filthy Garments – Zechariah 3:3-4

Death – Romans 6:23

ISAIAH 53:6

20

Tempted and Tried

In the Bible, temptation is a test of faith and obedience. It never comes from God leading us into sin, but it is often the result of the broken world we deal with every day. Followers of Jesus are called to stay alert, pray, and depend on God's Spirit and the truth of Scripture to overcome those moments when Satan is on the attack.

...Temptation is present in our lives as a test of our faith and loyalty to God.

...God allows testing but does not entice people to evil as a divine speed trap.

...Scripture calls us to resist temptation by relying on God's strength.

...Through Christ, followers find the power to resist temptation.

In the Lord's Prayer, we are taught to ask God to deliver us from evil rather than leading us into temptation.

MATTHEW 6:9-13

21

Satan's Resumé

Deceiver – The father of lies. (John 8:44)

Accuser – The accuser of the brothers and sisters. (Revelation 12:10)

Tempter – Sets traps for followers of Jesus. (1 Thessalonians 3:5)

Murderer & Destroyer – John gives him the title of "abaddon" the destroyer. (Revelation 9:11)

Arrogant Rebel – He desired to exalt himself above God. (Isaiah 14:13-14)

Enemy & Opponent – The roaring lion ready to devour God's people and God's plan. (Matthew 13:39)

2 THESSALONIANS 2:4

22

Jesus, The Only High Priest We'll Ever Need

Jesus is not just another priest in a long list of priests. He is the final, perfect, and eternal High Priest who bridges the gap between God and people once and for all.

Not sure what to say to God or how to say it? Let Jesus represent you in the throne room of heaven as your High Priest. He is the ultimate mediator between a holy God and less-than holy people.

...Jesus is the perfect sacrifice.

...Jesus is the sinless mediator.

...Jesus establishes a permanent priesthood.

...Jesus gives us direct access to God's throne of grace.

HEBREWS 4:14-16

23

Who Is the Perfect Messiah?

Seven hundred years before Jesus was born, the prophet Isaiah gave a prophetic prediction of what the long-awaited Messiah would be like and what he would accomplish.

The virgin will conceive and call him Immanuel. (Isaiah 7:14)

A child is born, wonderful counselor, Mighty God. (Isaiah 9:6-7)

A shoot from the stump of Jesse. (Isaiah 11:2)

He will bring justice as my servant. (Isaiah 42:1-4)

I offered my back to those who beat me. (Isaiah 50:6)

Despised and pierced for our transgressions. (Isaiah 53:3-7)

The servant will be raised and lifted up. (Isaiah 52:13-15)

The Spirit of the Lord is upon me. (Isaiah 61:1-2)

He will swallow up death forever. (Isaiah 25:8)

Nations will come to your light. (Isaiah 60:1-3)

ISAIAH 53:1-12

24

What Does "Messiah" Mean?

In the Bible the word "messiah" comes from the Hebrew word *masiah*, typically defined as "the anointed one." In Greek, it is *christos* from which we get "Christ." So, Jesus the Christ means Jesus the Anointed One.

In the Old Testament, the term referred to someone anointed with oil for a special role. It was used for kings, priests, or prophets.

The New Testament introduces us to Jesus as the fulfillment of messianic prophecies throughout the Old Testament: a descendant of Abraham, From the Tribe of Judah, heir to David's throne, born of a virgin, born in Bethlehem, a light to the nations, ministry of healing, rejected by his own people, betrayed by a close friend, silent before his accusers, pierced and wounded, crucified with criminals, no broken bones, buried with the rich, resurrection from the dead, and ascension and eternal reign.

Altogether, biblical scholars have identified over 300 prophecies about the Messiah that are fulfilled in Jesus the Christ, Jesus the Anointed One.

**JOHN 1:41;
MATTHEW 16:16**

25

Spiritual Strongholds

Satan's strongholds - Refer to spiritual obstacles that must be torn down: false beliefs, lies, pride, worldly philosophies that resist God's truth. Satan uses these and other addictive strongholds to keep people captive.

God's strongholds - Refer to God as protector offering a fortified place of safety. Psalm 9:9 says, "The Lord is a refuge for the oppressed, a stronghold in times of trouble." See also: Psalm 18:2; Nahum 1:7; Proverbs 21:22.

2 CORINTHIANS 10:3-5

26

Jesus' Emotional Intelligence

Compassion means being deeply moved by the suffering of others and being moved to act on their behalf.

Jesus had compassion toward the sick. (Mark 1:41; Matthew 14:14)

Jesus had compassion toward the hungry. (Matthew 15:32)

Jesus had compassion toward those in grief. (Luke 7:13)

Jesus had compassion toward the spiritually lost. (Matthew 9:36)

Jesus' compassion shows his emotional intelligence, in both sympathy and empathy. Sympathy is feeling **for** someone. Empathy is feeling **with** someone not just **for** someone. Jesus' compassion led to seeing the need, feeling the pain, and taking some action. He is an example for every follower: "For we do not have a high priest who is unable to empathize with our weaknesses, but we have one who has been tempted in every way, just as we are – yet he did not sin."

HEBREWS 4:15

27

Following Jesus Is a Collaborative Sport

The Apostle Paul uses the phrase "one another" to describe how Jesus' followers are called to live in community. Some say there are fifty-nine "one another" statements in the Bible. Christianity isn't for sole contributors; It's about living in community!

A few examples:

Love One Another. (1 Peter 1:22)

Live in Harmony With One Another. (Romans 12:16)

In Humility Toward One Another. (1 Peter 5:5)

Encourage One Another. (1 Thessalonians 5:11)

Don't Slander One Another. (James 4:11)

HEBREWS 4:15

28

The Whole Is More than the Sum of its Parts

Our bodies have many different parts that work together. Each part has a unique function. When we have pain in one part of the body it affects the entire body. In the letter to the church in the city of Corinth, the Apostle Paul used the image of a human body to describe the local church. The analogy is a reminder of how the church works together:

Unity in Diversity – Different gifts serve the same purpose

Interdependence – No part can say it doesn't need the other parts.

Mutual Care – When one part suffers, the whole body feels it

Christ is the Head – Jesus guides the church and sustains its mission while followers grow in faith and build one another up in Christ.

1 CORINTHIANS 12:12-27

29

Old Faithful

Yes, it's the famous cone geyser in Yellowstone National Park. It was named in 1870. It erupts reliably every 44 to 120 minutes. Even more amazing is the God who created it. He is the original Old Faithful! He keeps his promises. His character never changes. His love endures forever. God's faithfulness is the foundation of our trust and hope in him.

Our faithfulness to God is a fruit of the Holy Spirit's work in and through us. It reflects our loyalty, dependability, and steadfast love toward God and other people in our life. It' not about believing but about living out our trust in God through consistent obedience to him and personal integrity with people.

1 CORINTHIANS 1:9

30

Amazing Grace

Grace is God's unearned favor and kindness to us. It's not something we can achieve or purchase. It's a gift. It's God giving us what we could never earn or deserve. Why is it so amazing?

...It is counterintuitive to the way our world works.

...It forgives the unforgiveable

...It changes lives

...It is unending

...It bridges the gap between a holy God and not-so-holy people

...It offers hope of a second chance to the hopeless

EPHESIANS 2:8-9

31

Who's Your Bestie?

Jesus' ministry strategy was to send people out two by two. The book of Luke records, "After this the Lord appointed seventy-two others and sent them two by two ahead of him to go to every town and place where he was about to go" (Luke 10:1).

Serving two by two reflects God's design for ministry as a partnership. Teams provide encouragement, strength, accountability, and diversity of style and personality. In the wisdom literature in the Old Testament book of Ecclesiastes, the writer says: "Two are better than one, because they have a good return for their labor. If either of them falls down, one can help the other up. But pity anyone who falls and has no one to help them up."

ECCLESIASTES 4:9-10

APRIL

GOODNESS OF GOD

"For the Lord is good and his love endures forever; his faithfulness continues through all generations."

— PSALM 100:5

Goodness of God

I love you, Lord
Oh, your mercy never failed me
All my days, I've been held in your hands
From the moment that I wake up
Until I lay my head
Oh, I will sing of the goodness of God

I love your voice
You have led me through the fire
And in darkest night you are close like no other
I've known you as a Father
I've known you as a Friend
And I have lived in the goodness of God,

And all my life you have been faithful,
And all my life you have been so, so good
With every breath that I am able
Oh, I will sing of the goodness of God, yeah!

And all my life you have been faithful
And all my life you have been so, so good
With every breath that I am able
Oh, I'm gonna sing of the goodness of God[6]

01

April Fools' Day

Mercy describes God's compassionate forgiveness toward us even in our most foolish moments. Once we grasp the depth of love behind God's forgiveness of us, we learn the harder lesson of paying it forward to others. Have fun today doing some foolish pranks to irritate your family, friends, or coworkers, but this day isn't just a day for harmless pranks against others. It's a reminder that we can offer others what God offers us. The price is minimal compared to the ransom God paid to rescue us from the prison of sin. God's mercy is undeserved but freely given. How can we do any less in our relationships with family, friends, neighbors, and co-workers?

*"At one time we too were foolish, disobedient, deceived,
and enslaved by all kinds of passions and pleasures...
But when the kindness and love of God our Savior appeared,
he saved us, not because of righteous things we had done,
but because of his mercy."*

TITUS 3:3-5

02

The Levels of Forgiveness

Forgiveness is a dynamic process that unfolds in stages. People can get stuck in any stage if left to their own emotions, strengths, ability, or will. What follows are not linear steps to forgive but steps along the way of forgiving in a variety of orders.

1. I acknowledge the hurt.

2. I decide to forgive.

3. I forgive, but I still hold on to my resentment.

4. I forgive if the other person apologizes.

5. I forgive regardless of their response in order to free myself from resentment and the need for revenge.

6. I forgive is to reconcile the relationship out of respect to the other and for the sake of family and friends around us yet not fully restoring the relationship to what it once was.

7. I forgive as an act of grace and mercy in order to actively rebuild and restore the relationship, if it's safe, appropriate, and reciprocal.

Followers of Jesus understand that forgiveness of another is our response to God's forgiveness of us. Jesus told Peter to forgive seventy times seven, showing that forgiveness has no limit, Matthew 18:21-22. Following Jesus makes each stage of forgiveness possible. Level #7 may not be humanly possible given your story or theirs. It may not be wise. It may not be safe. It may not happen on this side of eternity.

COLOSSIANS 3:13

03

Telling Lies

The Bible is clear about lying. It's one of the Ten Commandments: "Do not bear false witness against your neighbor." In writing to the church at Colossae, Paul writes: "Do not lie to one another, since you have put off the old self with its practices" (Colossians 3:9). Lies may save us from short-term awkwardness, but later on the consequences negatively compound exponentially.

...Lies erode trust in relationships.

...Lies require more lying to cover up the truth.

...Lies may cause harm long term relational damage or dysfunction.

...Lies damage credibility and then it can take years to restore one's character.

...Confession and making amends can begin the path to restoration in any relationship.

EPHESIANS 4:25

04

The Rhythm of Rest

The Sabbath Principle sets one day in seven aside for rest and restoration: mentally, emotionally, physically, and spiritually. It's the original value of living with a work-life balance. God modeled it in creation when he rested on the seventh day, not because he was tired, but to establish a rhythm for humanity and all of creation. The changes in how work gets done in our increasingly busy lives makes the Fourth Commandment nearly impossible: "Remember the Sabbath day and keep it holy" (Exodus 20:8).

Practices of a holy Sabbath:

...Find ways to pause from normal work and busyness.

...Some families opt for Saturday night church in order to keep Sunday as an entire day for family and rest.

...Spend unhurried time with God in prayer, worship, and Scripture.

...Make space for physical rest and family relationships.

...Give the gift of rest to family members, employees, even creation itself.

...Discuss Sabbath rest with your family and agree to basic commitments for this one day in seven.

EXODUS 20:8-11

05

Why Did Miracles Happen

Miracles are supernatural acts of God that interrupt the natural order of our world to demonstrate God's identity and power as well as to meet human needs. God's power is for God's purposes:

To authenticate Jesus' identity as God in human flesh.

To demonstrate God's compassion for people in need.

To reveal God's power pointing people to faith.

To advance the work of God's Kingdom by showing his rule over sickness and death.

To confirm the message of the Gospel and build the early church.

JOHN 20:30-31

06

How to Pray Like Jesus – Part One

"When you pray, don't be like the hypocrites who love to pray publicly on street corners and in the synagogues where everyone can see them. I tell you the truth, that is all the reward they will ever get. But when you pray, go away by yourself, shut the door behind you, and pray to your Father in private. Then your Father, who sees everything, will reward you" (Matthew 6:5-6).

"When you pray, don't babble on and on as the Gentiles do. They think their prayers are answered merely by repeating their words again and again. Don't be like them, for your Father knows exactly what you need even before you ask him" (Matthew 6:7-8).

Two guidelines to remember from this Scripture:

1. Don't pray to impress others.
2. Don't assume the more words you use, the more likely it is that God will listen and answer.

MATTHEW 6:5-15

07

How to Pray Like Jesus – Part Two

Jesus said, "Pray like this: Our Father in heaven, may your name be kept holy. May your Kingdom come soon. May your will be done on earth, as it is in heaven. Give us today the food we need, and forgive us our sins, as we have forgiven those who sin against us. And lead us not into temptation but deliver us from the evil one" (Matthew 6:13).

The doxology, found in the book of Matthew and added at the end of the Lord's prayer in some manuscripts says, "For thine is the Kingdom, and the power, and the glory, forever. Amen" (Matthew 6:13). Praying each part of the Lord's prayer means that following Jesus is all about living in God's Kingdom not yours, doing that through God's power not yours, and following Jesus for God's glory not yours.

MATTHEW 6:9-13

08

Is the Bible Enough?

Scripture is complete, authoritative, and final. To add or subtract from it distorts its truth and undermines its authority. Other holy books that add to it or reinterpret its meaning and application can be misleading and must be judged according to the standard of truth in the Bible. When there is disagreement, always default to the Bible.

At the end of John's vision in the book of Revelation, he includes this: "I warn everyone who hears the words of the prophecy of this scroll: If anyone adds anything to them, God will add to that person the plagues described in this scroll. And if anyone takes words away from this scroll of prophecy, God will take away from that person any share in the tree of life and in the Holy City which are described in this scroll" (Revelation 22:18-19).

DEUTERONOMY 4:2;
PROVERBS 30:5-6

09

Life Verses #2 –
God Works for Good

"And we know that in all things God works for the good of those who love him, who have been called according to his purpose" (Romans 8:28).

God is Sovereign - Nothing is wasted from God's perspective. He works through all things for the ultimate good of those who choose to love him.

Our Calling and His Purpose - The promise in this verse is directed to Christ followers who are called according to God's purpose for them.

Transformation - God's good is defined as being conformed to the image of Christ, not just God giving you favorable circumstances.

Christ Is Our Model - Followers are being transformed into the likeness of Christ.

Do you love God? Do you know your calling? Are you becoming more like Jesus?

ROMANS 8:28

10

Old Hundredth

A paraphrase and hymn of Psalm 100 by William Kethe in 1561[7]

All people that on earth do dwell,
Sing to the Lord with cheerful voice;
Him serve with mirth, His praise forth tell,
Come ye before Him and rejoice.
Know that the Lord is God indeed;
Without our aid he did us make;
We are His folk, he doth us feed,
And for His sheep he doth us take.
O enter then his gates with praise;
Approach with joy his courts unto;
Praise, laud, and bless his Name always,
For it is seemly so to do.

For why? The Lord our God is good,
His mercy is forever sure;
His truth at all times firmly stood,
And shall from age to age endure.
To Father, Son, and Holy Ghost,
The God whom heaven and earth adore,
From men and from the angel host
Be praise and glory evermore. Amen.

PSALM 100

11

Worship Is Worth-ship

Worship means to give God the honor, reverence, and the devotion he alone deserves. Worship is directed to God alone – not to people, angels, or idols.

- We can worship privately – Prayer, meditation, and personal praise. (Psalm 63:1-4)

- We can worship corporately – Gathering with other followers of Jesus to honor God. (Acts 2:42-47)

- We can worship in the way we live – Offering every part of life to God. (Romans 12:1)

JOHN 4:23-24

12

Life Verses #3 – God's Gotta Plan

The Old Testament prophet, Jeremiah, sent a letter to the Jewish exiles living in Babylon after Jerusalem was conquered. God told them that their captivity would last seventy years, but he had not forgotten about them. God's message through Jeremiah: "For I know the plans I have for you," declares the Lord, "plans to prosper you and not to harm you, plans to give you hope and a future."

God's plan referred to what God would do after these seventy years. He would bring them back from exile to their homeland in Jerusalem and restore their lives and the city. For us, it is a reminder of God's purposeful character. He is not, nor is he ever, random. Even in our hardest times, God's intentions are for our good, our hope, and our future!

He has a purpose and a plan and a timeline for you.

JEREMIAH 29:11

13

The Strategy of a Great Leader

Nehemiah was living in exile, away from his home in Jerusalem. He longed to return home, but even more, he was concerned about the condition of his hometown: "Come, let us rebuild the wall of Jerusalem, and we will no longer be in disgrace." His leadership was grounded in faith in God and service to people, while facing the impossible.

...**Nehemiah had a vision.** Great leaders connect their team to a higher purpose than themselves.

...**Nehemiah realized his dependence on God.** Prayer anchored his leadership as he sought God's direction at every step in the process of rebuilding the wall around Jerusalem.

...**Nehemiah was strategic.** He surveyed the project quietly at night to gather all the facts before organizing the people for the project. Careful preparation always precedes action.

...**Nehemiah involved everyone.** Every household worked on a section of the wall near their own homes to create ownership and unity.

...**Nehemiah effectively dealt with his critics.** He never lost focus on the mission.

...**Nehemiah had integrity.** He never exploited people for his own personal gain but set an example of generosity.

...**Nehemiah has a greater motivation in mind.** Once the wall was completed, he focused on the spiritual renewal of the people (Nehemiah 8-10).

NEHEMIAH 2:17

14

You Were Created as a Masterpiece

In spite of whatever was going on in David's life in the Old Testament, he was aware that God knew everything about him before he was born: "For you created my inmost being; you knit me together in my mother's womb. I praise you because I am fearfully and wonderfully made; your works are wonderful, I know that full well. My frame was not hidden from you when I was made in the secret place, when I was woven together in the depths of the earth. Your eyes saw my unformed body; all the days ordained for me were written in your book before one of them came to be" (Psalm 139:13-16).

In God's eyes, you are a work of art, a person skillfully crafted in God's own image, a masterpiece of the Creator. Who cares what anyone else thinks!

Fearfully means you were created with awe-inspiring reverence.

Wonderfully emphasize your uniqueness and excellence.

No wonder Paul says in writing to the followers of Christ in the city of Ephesus: "For we are God's masterpiece. He has created us anew in Christ Jesus, so we can do the good things he planned for us long ago."

EPHESIANS 2:10

15

Make Room for the Next Generation

In the early church, Peter is describing the Pentecost when the Holy Spirit was given to Jesus' followers just as Jesus had promised. The Holy Spirit would dwell in them even as Jesus had been with them. Peter connects it all to an Old Testament prophecy from Joel about the outpouring of God's Spirit.

"And afterward, I will pour out my Spirit on all people. Your sons and daughters will prophecy, your old men will dream dreams, your young men will see visions. Even on my servants, both men and women, I will pour out my Spirit in those days" (Joel 2:28-29).

This announcement was, and is, something that applies to all people regardless of age or gender. It's for sons and daughters. It's for young and old. It's for all who serve as followers of Jesus. Prophecy is not primarily about foretelling the future. More often the word prophecy is about "forth-telling" or speaking God's truth into the present day. The prophecy of Joel was written about 800 years before the birth of Jesus. He was declaring a new thing God would eventually be doing. He announced and welcomed old and young, men and women to the opportunity to proclaim God's truth to the world. We are better together in this heavenly assignment across generations and genders.

JOEL 2:28-29

16

Family Dysfunction Goes Really Bad

Jacob had a house mostly full of boys. Joseph was number eleven. He was Jacob's favorite and got the fancy clothes to prove it to the other kids in the family. The coat of many colors in Genesis 37:3 was an irritating reminder to the rest of them. Their jealousy turned to hatred.

When Joseph was 17, they plotted against him. The coat dripped in blood was their defense to their father, as if Joseph had been killed by a wild animal. He was sold to a caravan of traders heading to Egypt.

But that is not the end of the story. Joseph was eventually promoted by Pharoah as his second in command over all of Egypt. When Jacob and family found themselves in the middle of a famine, the sons headed to Egypt to get food for their survival. Who was in charge? Joseph. It's an amazing and dramatic story of reconciliation and forgiveness!

God gives hope to even the most dysfunctional of families when he has the opportunity to finish their story. He certainly did that for Joseph. He honors us when we demonstrate the kind of faithfulness Joseph had through the worst and best of what life deals us. How about your family? Listen to Joseph's words as a rare and uncommon demonstration of the kind of love and forgiveness that only comes from God. "You meant evil against me, but God meant it for good, to bring it about that many people should be kept alive" (Genesis 50:20).

GENESIS 37–50

17

Talking to God

Prayer is talking to God. Anyone can do it. It's not limited to a set formula as in the Lord's Prayer. We can use any words, have silent thoughts, or even the posture of your heart is a prayer to God.

A well-rounded prayer includes the following **ACTS** acronym:

Adoration – Celebrating God for who he is.

Confession – Seeking God's forgiveness by admitting when we have messed up.

Thanksgiving – Gratitude for all of God's blessings.

Supplication – Asking for help or guidance for yourself or for another.

Prayer is both talking to God and listening for his guidance. It is just like good communication with your family or best friend. It is both a privilege and a necessity. This is how we stay connected to God.

**PHILIPPIANS 4:6;
PSALM 46:10**

18

Letting Others into Your Life

Pastors – Focus on our spiritual life and relationship with God. They offer teaching, encouragement, and prayer.

Mentors – Focus on an experienced-based guidance to others. They share wisdom learned in their own life and career. They offer advice, perspective, and role modeling.

Coaches – Focus primarily on performance growth in specific goals. They help clarify goals, identify obstacles, and develop strategies. They are question driven drawing answers out of you empowering you to move forward.

Therapists – Focus primarily on mental health, emotional well-being, and healing from trauma. They provide clinical treatment for psychological issues using evidence-based methods to bring healing and offer coping skills.

Teachers – Focus on knowledge transfer. They explain concepts and provide instructions to inform but do not always focus on personal development and application as coaches, mentors, pastors, and therapists do.

The lesson in this list is to know who to confide in, when, and why. If the connection and fit does not work then move on.

PROVERBS 27:17

19

Meditation Is Time for You

It is the practice of training your mind to focus, to be present, and to develop awareness. It's about quieting the constant overstimulation of thoughts and ideas every hour of every day. This is about your own intentionality of thoughts not the bombardment of ideas from others.

Sabbath is your designated time to be still and alone with your thoughts.

Sanctuary is your designated place to be alone for brief or extended times of meditation.

Awareness is your practice in meditation helping you notice thoughts and feelings without being controlled by them.

Meditation is an experience that reduces stress and anxiety. It improves focus and mental clarity. It can be one way to enhance your spiritual growth.

PSALM 1:2

20

The Practices of
Spiritual Disciplines

Disciplines are intentional practices that help a person grow closer to God, deepen their faith, and cultivate a life shaped by spiritual maturity.

Prayer – Talking with God through praise, confession, thanksgiving, and petition.

Bible Reading – Engaging Scripture not just to know more but to apply its wisdom and become more Christlike in every area of life.

Fasting – Abstaining from food or other things (television or internet) to focus that time on God and expressing dependence on him.

Silence and Solitude – Pulling away from the noise of the world's distractions to listen for God's leadings and promptings.

Confession and Repentance – Displaying honesty before God or another while seeking renewal and growth.

1 TIMOTHY 4:7-8

21

Life Verses #4: –
If I, Can I, Will I?

"If we confess our sins, God is faithful and just and will forgive us our sins and purify us from all unrighteousness" (1 John 1:9).

My Confession
Agreeing with God about my sin. Then I take responsibility for it and turn 180 degrees away from it.

God's Faithfulness
He keeps his promises. It is the essence of his character.

God's Justice
Forgiveness is rooted in Jesus' work on the cross that satisfies God's commitment to justice for all.

My Cleansing
When sins are forgiven, our hearts are made clean, and our fellowship with God is restored.

1 JOHN 1:8-10

22

Old Testament Names for God –
Part One

Elohim – God's power as Creator (Genesis 1:1)

Yahweh – The name of Jehovah means Lord. It is God's covenant name, "I AM." (Exodus 3:14-15)

Adonai – Lord, Master points to God's authority. (Psalm 8:1)

El Shaddai – God Almighty. Shows his sufficiency and power. (Genesis 17:1)

El Elyon – God Most High stresses God's supremacy. (Genesis 14:18-20)

El Roi – The God Who Sees. (Genesis 16:13)

Yahweh - Jireh – The Lord Will Provide. (Genesis 22:14)

No wonder the Psalmist says, "The Lord is my Shepherd, I have all that I need." (Psalm 23:1)

DEUTERONOMY 6:4

23

Old Testament Names for God – Part Two

Yahweh-Rapha – The Lord who heals. (Exodus 15:26)

Yahweh-Nissi – The Lord is my banner. (Exodus 17:15)

Yahweh-Shalom – The Lord is peace. (Judges 6:24)

Yahweh-Raha – The Lord is my shepherd. (Psalm 23:1)

Yahweh-Tsidkenu – The Lord our righteousness. (Jeremiah 23:6)

Yahweh-Shammah – The Lord is there. (Ezekiel 48:35)

DEUTERONOMY 6:4

24

New Testament Names for God - Part One

Theos – Greek word for "God." (Matthew 1:23)

Kurios – Lord pointing to his authority. (Philippians 2:11)

Pater – Father revealing his intimacy in relationships. (Matthew 6:9)

Abba – Aramaic for "Daddy, Father." (Romans 8:15; Galatians 4:6)

Immanuel – God with us. (Matthew 1:23)

DEUTERONOMY 6:4

25

The New Testament Names for God – Part Two

Logos – The Word. (John 1:1)

Christos – Christ, the Anointed One. (John 1:41)

Soter – Savior. (Luke 2:11)

Pantokrator – Almighty. (Revelation 1:8)

Alpha and Omega – Beginning and End. (Revelation 22:13)

God is the Creator, Sustainer, Provider, Healer, Shepherd, Righteous Judge, Savior, and Ever-Present Father.

DEUTERONOMY 6:4

26

When It's Okay to Be Sad

Lamentations is included in the Old Testament as a collection of five poems written after the destruction of the city of Jerusalem by the Babylonians in 586 B.C. The tone of the poems is one of grief, mourning, and sorrow, balanced by themes of faith and hope in God's mercy.

Poem #1 – Jerusalem's Desolation

Poem #2 – God's Judgment

Poem #3 – A Personal Cry

Poem #4 – Before and After of the city

Poem #5 – Prayer for Restoration

It is assumed to have been written by Jeremiah as he addresses sorrow over Israel's sin of turning away from God. Then he touches on human suffering and its pain and loss. Even in suffering, God's steadfast love continues as Jeremiah finds hope in God's mercy. He is honest in describing the tension between God's justice and his compassion.

We learn in Lamentations that it is okay to have times of sadness with a realization that God is already there to move us through that season to a time of hope that only he can offer.

LAMENTATIONS 3:22-23

27

Love Songs

Song of Songs or Song of Solomon is a collection of love poems expressed between a bride and her bridegroom. It celebrates romantic love, passion, intimacy, and commitment. The writing moves among three voices: the man, the woman, and a chorus of friends or daughters of Jerusalem.

Some interpret the book literally – A celebration of marital love.

Some interpret it allegorically – An allegory of God's love for Israel.

Some interpret it devotionally – A picture of believers' relationship with God.

Are you in love? What can you learn from Solomon?

SONG OF SOLOMON 8:6-7

28

Dealing with Differentness

Peter had a vison (Acts 10:9-16; 11:4-10). He saw a sheet filled with things that were considered unclean under Jewish law. In the vision, he was told to eat but refused because of their laws. Three times it happened, and he was told in the vision, "Do not call anything impure that God has made clean" (Acts 10:15).

The vision was God's way of showing Peter that the Gospel message of Jesus' death and resurrection was good news for all people, not just the Jews. There was a group among the Jewish people called Judaizers who taught that Gentiles (non-Jews) must first become Jewish before they could truly be considered a follower of Jesus. For them, it meant the Gentiles must be circumcised.

A meeting was scheduled in Jerusalem recorded in Acts 15:1-29. The Judaizers were there to reinforce this requirement. Then Peter shared his vision and the message from God. Peter said that God's salvation is through the grace of Jesus, and we are all saved in the same way. James, the brother of Jesus, stood and said, "We should not make it difficult for the Gentiles who are turning to God."

It's easy in our faith traditions today to add "extra requirements" people must do to be a genuine follower of Jesus like we are. Let's keep it simple. Jesus died for our sins. He was resurrected to demonstrate God's power over the enemy of death. He invites us to follow his teaching and his example. Period. Nothing more. Nothing less. Let's not make it difficult for people to find and follow Jesus.

ACTS 1:19

29

400 Years of Slavery

The story of the Exodus is the story of God's deliverance of the Israelites from slavery in Egypt under the leadership of Moses. They had been in Egypt since the days of Joseph and his brothers in Genesis 37-50. The story of Moses and the Exodus is a familiar one, especially the visuals of the 12 plagues God brought down on the Pharoah who refused to let his free labor of all the Israelites leave Egypt.

The story continues in crossing through God's parting of the Red Sea. God establishes his new Covenant relationship with the nation at Mount Sinai. Then the forty-year walk to the promised land that could have only taken forty days. The consequences of stubborn people.

Perhaps all these connections represent one of the most memorable parts of the Old Testament. The Exodus story contains spiritual truth for every generation since.

...God is still in the business of delivering people from all varieties of bondage.

...God is still in the business of calling people into a unique relationship with himself.

...God is always near even if we choose to be far.

...Jesus became the forever Moses who offers deliverance to anyone.

EXODUS 14:13-14

30

Shepherds? At Bethlehem?
Jesus First Guests? Really?

Shepherds were among the lowest social classes in ancient Israel. They were poor, uneducated, and often living on the fringes of society. That is not surprising as they were out in the fields all alone with the sheep. When the angels first appeared to these shepherds to announce the birth of Jesus, God demonstrated that the good news of salvation is for everyone, not just the powerful or religious elite.

God's choice of shepherds reflects his favor toward humility and the simplicity of one's heart. Jesus later described himself as "the Good Shepherd who lays down his life for the sheep" (John 10:11). After seeing the newborn Christ, the shepherds were the first witnesses and messengers of the gospel. They "spread the word concerning what had been told them" (Luke 2:7).

The shepherds story shows that God's glory shines brightest in our humility. Luke added: "He has brought down rulers from their thrones but has lifted up the humble."

LUKE 1:52

MAY

HOW GREAT IS OUR GOD

"Lift up your eyes and look to the heavens: Who created all these? He who brings out the starry host one by one and calls forth each of them by name. Because of his great power and mighty strength, not one of them is missing"

— ISAIAH 40:26

How Great Is Our God

The splendor of a King, clothed in majesty
Let all the earth rejoice
All the earth rejoice
He wraps himself in Light, and darkness tries to hide
And trembles at his voice
Trembles at his voice

Age to age he stands
And time is in his hands
Beginning and the end
Beginning and the end

The Godhead Three in One
Father, Spirit and Son
The Lion and the Lamb
The Lion and the Lamb

How great is our God
Sing with me how great is our God
And all will see how great
How great is our God

Name above all names
You are worthy of our praise
And my heart will sing
How great is our God

How great is our God
Sing with me how great is our God
And all will see how great
How great is our God[8]

01

Dollars and Sense

The Bible talks more about money, possessions, and stewardship in 2000+ verses than any other topic. The tithe is one of the money topics it defines as ten percent of one's income. How does that work out in real life? Consider the financial principles that guide a follower of Jesus:

Give according to your means. (2 Corinthians 8:1-5)

Save proportionately. (1 Corinthians 16:2)

Give willingly and cheerfully. (2 Corinthians 9:7)

Share with regular consistency. (1 Corinthians 16:2)

Be generous. (Proverbs 14:21, 31; 19:17)

Sacrifice as God prospers you. (Mark 2:42-44; 2 Corinthians 8:3)

The "10-10-80 rule" is a simple way to manage or steward your financial resources, and it works:

- Give 10%
- Save 10%
- Spend 80%.

LUKE 12:48

02

Is It Ever Okay to Get Mad?

Anger is a normal human emotion. Under your control, it can serve a purpose. Out of your control, it can ruin your life or another's.

Righteous anger. It is in line with God's understanding of restoring justice. It occurs when people are in situations where they are being unfairly hurt by others.

Sinful anger. It occurs as a result of one's selfish, self-centered attitudes that lead to negative words and behaviors.

>...The Apostle Paul says, "In your anger do not sin" (Ephesians 4:26).

>...The writer of Proverbs 29:11 adds, "Fools give full vent to their rage, but the wise bring calm in the end."

>...The brother of Jesus includes one final suggestion in James 1:19-20: "Be slow to anger."

Pride can keep the person who lives in anger from reaching out for help. If your life is littered with anger damage in the lives of people who used to love you, then in humility, reach out for professional guidance. It will help you build new relational and emotional habits that will change the course of your life. You will never regret getting professional help to become a new and better person. You never have to apologize for things you leave unsaid. Resting in peace (RIP) is the result of repairing all things broken before your last and final breath on this side of eternity.

NUMBERS 14:18

03

Two Non-negotiables of Christ-like Character

Integrity. How others see you. It's the intrapersonal side of Christ-like character. Proverbs 10:9 says, "Whoever walks in integrity walks securely, but whoever takes crooked paths will be found out."

Respect. How you see others. It's the interpersonal side of Christ-like character. In Philippians 2:3-4, Paul writes, "Do nothing out of selfish ambition or vain conceit. Rather, in humility value others above yourselves, not looking to your own interests but each of you to the interests of others."

Want to be like Jesus? It's all about how you see others and how they see you.

PROVERBS 22:1

04

The Ministry of Being There

Anyone can just show up. You don't have to say anything or do anything. Just show up when others need you. Your presence brings comfort and demonstrates compassion. Quiet compassionate companionship will genuinely minister to a friend, a co-worker, or a family member in a time of need.

Just be you. Just be with them. Just do it.

ROMANS 12:15

05

Parenting That Breaks a Child's Spirit

When the Apostle Paul writes to parents in the church in Colossae, he says this: "Do not embitter your children, or they will become discouraged" (Colossians 3:21).

Embitter has three shades of meaning for any parent:

    ...To provoke repeatedly.
    ...To irritate over time.
    ...To stir up resentment through constant pressure.

Embittered parenting isn't about one bad parenting day. It is about a chronic tone of repeated sharpness and relentless correction. It's a pattern that poisons the parent – child relationship. They may be compliant until they can leave your control, but one day they will leave and never look back. It's not too late to learn to improve your parenting and the child's spirit you are shaping.

Discouraged literally means:

    ...To lose heart.
    ...To lose inner motivation.
    ...To become emotionally weary.
    ...To give up inwardly

A discouraged child doesn't fight. They are probably not allowed to. A discouraged child withdraws. It is about the collapse of their inner spirit when they conclude that they will never satisfy the expectations of their parents. The parent's behavior results in the child's inner state. Parents can be right and still damage their child's heart. It is all about how authority is exercised. Repeated harshness doesn't produce obedience. It results in the loss of heart. James was the brother of Jesus who led the first church in Jerusalem. Read his advice as a place to start in changing your approach to parenting imperfect children.

JAMES 1:19

06

Hallelujah

The word comes from the Hebrew word "hallel" which means praise and the word "Yah" which is short for Yahweh (God), so hallelujah literally means Praise Yahweh or Praise God.

God is praised for his greatness, (Psalm 150:1-6).

God is praised for his faithfulness, (Psalm 146:1-2).

God is praised for his works in creation, (Psalm 148:1-5)

"Hallelujah! For the Lord our God the Almighty reigns."

REVELATION 19:1-6

07

Would Jesus Have Picked You for His Team?

Jesus chose twelve to be his closest followers and to carry on his mission after his resurrection. **Peter**, also called Simon Peter was a fisherman, **Andrew**, was also a fisherman, **James**, was the brother of John, **John**, also a son of Zebedee, **Philip** was from Bethsaida, **Bartholomew**, was also called Nathanael, **Matthew**, was also called Levi, **Thomas**, was also called Didymus, **James**, was the son of Alphaeus often called James the Less, **Thaddeus**, was also called Jude, **Simon** was known as **The Zealot**, and **Judas Iscariot** would eventually betray Jesus. After Judas's death, he was replaced by **Matthias**.

Jesus also had many other followers and friends like Lazarus and his two sisters, Mary and Martha. There were seventy or so who were sent out two by two including the twelve in Luke 10. All were unique with individual personalities and peculiarities. They hardly represented the most likely to succeed in their graduating classes. They often seemed to miss the point in understanding Jesus' teaching, and they were not unusual in their competitive spirit vying for positions of prominence in their assumptions about Jesus' Kingdom. Yes, you and I would have fit in rather well.

God always does the extraordinary through ordinary people just like you and me.

**LUKE 6:13-16;
ACTS 1:13**

08

Mary, the Mother of Jesus

Mary's story shows how God often works through unnoticed people with willing hearts. She demonstrates humility, availability, courage, and deep faith. We see Mary at the key biblical moments in Jesus' life and teaching, even standing near the cross when Jesus was crucified (John19:25-27). Mary is a fulfillment of prophecy that a "virgin will conceive and give birth to a son" (Isaiah 7:14).

Mary is an example of faith but not an object of faith. She never asked people to honor her, but she always directed attention to Jesus. (Luke 1:46-55). The Bible is clear that worship is reserved for God alone: Matthew 4:10; Isaiah 42:8. There is a distinct difference between honoring someone and worshipping someone. In Luke 11:27-28, a woman cried out: "Blessed is the mother who gave you birth and nursed you." Jesus replied: "Blessed rather are those who hear the word of God and obey it." He honored his mother but emphasized that obedience to God is what should be celebrated.

LUKE 1:38

09

Joseph Was Just the Dad

Joseph was the earthly adoptive father of Jesus who also demonstrated a humble obedience to God's request to take Mary as his wife. He did it in spite of the Jewish laws of the day which would have prohibited it. He did it in spite of her potential embarrassment to his own reputation with friends and family. See Matthew 1:18-25. He was a carpenter in order to provide for his family. He taught Jesus his trade while raising Jesus in a faithful Jewish household.

We read little of Joseph during Jesus' public ministry. Some suggest he may have died before Jesus started teaching and ministering publicly. He is remembered for his availability to God, his humility, and his obedience in listening to God's leading throughout the birth story and early days in Jesus' life. Let's not forget the example of the Dad when we pay so much more attention to the Mom.

MATTHEW 1:19

10

Angels Are Part of the Heavenly Host

Angels are spiritual beings created by God to serve him and carry out his will. See Psalm 148:2 and Colossians 1:16. The meaning of "angel" in both the Hebrew and Greek languages is "messenger."

Some are Archangels. Others are Cherubim or Seraphim. They are powerful, holy beings who worship God, deliver his messages, protect his people, and engage in spiritual battles, while always pointing to God's glory, not their own.

Their roles:

Messengers – Luke 1:26-38; Luke 2:8-14

Protectors – Psalm 91:11; Daniel 6:22

Worshippers – Isaiah 6: 1-3; Revelation 4:8

Ministers – Hebrews 1:14, Luke 22:43

**HEBREWS 13:2;
MATTHEW 18:10**

11

Our Struggle Is Against Spiritual Forces of Evil

These spiritual beings, sometimes called demons or unclean spirits, are often linked to Satan and his rebellion against God. They are generally understood as fallen angels, Revelation 12:7-9. They promote idolatry, sin, and rebellion against God.

...Jesus' death and resurrection disarmed spiritual powers, Colossians 2:15

...Followers of Jesus are warned to be watchful but assured of victory in Christ, Ephesians 6:10-12; James 4:7.

...Evil spirits will ultimately be judged and thrown into the lake of fire with Satan, Matthew 25:41; Revelation 20:10.

Even though we may face their influence in daily battles of the spirit in times of temptation, God has already won the war against Satan and all that is evil.

EPHESIANS 6:12

12

Warnings of Who Is in Trouble with God

There are warnings throughout the Bible of those who choose ways of living contrary to God's wisdom, Jesus' teaching, and the life he modeled.

The wicked and unrepentant – Psalm 1:4-6

The proud and arrogant – Proverbs 16:1

Those who reject God and his Word – John 3:36

The hypocrites – Isaiah 29:13

The oppressors – Isaiah 10:1-2

The immoral – I Corinthians 6:9-10

The lukewarm and spiritually indifferent – Revelation 3:15-16

God's story always balances warning with hope. Anyone who repents and turns to God finds forgiveness through Jesus Christ. (1 John 1:9)

ROMANS 10:9

13

Different Kinds of Prayers #1: Salvation

*"Lord Jesus,
I know that I am a sinner,
and I ask for your forgiveness.
I believe you died for my sins
and rose from the dead.
Today, I turn from my sins
and invite you into my life.
I trust you and choose to
follow you as my Savior and King.
Thank you for saving me.
Amen"*

ROMANS 10:9-10

14

Different kinds of Prayers #2: Thanksgiving

"Father in heaven,
I thank you for the gift of life today.
Thank you for my family, friends, and
every blessing you have given me.
I am grateful for your love, grace, and
mercy in sending Jesus to save me
from the consequences of sin.
Thank you for your promise to
never leave me or forget about me.
I know that every good and
perfect gift comes from you.
I am forever grateful.
In Jesus' name,
Amen."

1 THESSALONIANS 5:18

15

Different Kinds of Prayers #3: Intercession

"Lord God,
I lift up my family, friends, and
community to you today.
Please bring healing to those who are sick,
comfort those who are grieving,
and provide for those in need.
I pray for protection for those in danger.
I pray for wisdom for our leaders,
and I pray for strength for those who
lead your church to be a light in a dark world.
Most of all, draw our hearts closer to you,
that all may hear of your love and truth.
In Jesus' name,
Amen."

JOHN 17

16

Different Kinds of Prayers #4: Lament

"Oh Lord,
my heart is heavy, and I do not understand
why this trouble has come.
I feel overwhelmed and forgotten,
yet I know you are near.
How long must I wait for relief?
How long must I carry this sorrow?
Still, I will trust that you
hear my cries and hold my tears.
Be my refuge in the storm,
my comfort in the night,
and my strength when I am weak.
Though I do not see my way forward,
I claim your faithfulness and unfailing love.
Amen."

PSALM 13

17

Judgmental Psalms

One type of psalm included in the Old Testament is the imprecatory psalm. To imprecate means to invoke judgment, calamity, or a curse on someone. We all have those moments with a family member, co-worker, or toxic neighbor. These Psalms, included in the Old Testament collection, often express raw emotions of anger, grief, or the longing for God's justice when the writer or speaker has been mistreated or oppressed. See Psalms 35, 55, 59, 69, 109, 137, and 140.

Imprecatory Psalms acknowledge that God is not surprised or bothered when we bring the anguish of deep emotion in our cries for help and justice. They reflect the reality of our pain and our dependence on God to act justly on our behalf. In the best sense, they are our honest prayers, understanding that God will one day bring justice and judgment in his time and in his way.

DEUTERONOMY 32:35; ROMANS 12:19; PROVERBS 20:22; 1 THESSALONIANS 5:15

18

Eating Humble Pie

It's an idiom that means you are being forced to admit you were wrong, usually in a way this is embarrassing. Be careful of bold claims that prove to be wrong. Humility is a spiritual guardrail.

The Apostle Paul points us to Jesus: "In your relationships with one another, have the same mindset as Christ Jesus: Who, being in very nature God, did not consider equality with God something to be used to his own advantage; rather he made himself nothing by taking on the very nature of a servant, being made in human likeness. And being found in appearance as a man, he humbled himself by becoming obedient to death – even death on a cross" (Philippians 2:5-8).

It is insightfully said that humility isn't thinking less of yourself. It is thinking of yourself less.

JAMES 4:6

19

Attitudes Are Always Noticed

Attitudes are that inner mindset, the posture of one's heart that leads to our perspectives toward God, others, and life. Attitudes can lead to words that can result in behaviors, good, bad, or ugly.

Followers of Jesus understand that the right attitude flows from a heart transformed by the grace and mercy of God. When our heart is aligned with God's will, our attitudes reflect faith, hope, love, humility, and gratitude. These shape every relationship, every conversation, every decision, and every action.

PROVERBS 3:5

20

Non-Verbal Communication

Communication is more than what we say. Our body language speaks more loudly than any spoken word. Say one thing but your "non-verbal" communication says something else, and the message received in never what you said. When we communicate with clarity, our non-verbal communication matches the words we use.

Jesus invites us to communication clarity: "Let what you say be simply 'yes' or 'no' anything more than this comes from evil" (Matthew 5:37).

PROVERBS 6:12-14

21

Two Plus One Equals Three

"A cord of three strands is not easily broken" (Ecclesiastes 4:12). Followers of Jesus realize that every relationship potentially has a third strand:

Husband and wife plus God

Parent and child plus God

Child and parent plus God

You and a friend plus God

You and a neighbor plus God

You and a co-worker plus God

Leaving God out of every relationship changes it, and not for the better.

ECCLESIASTES 4:9-12

22

Faithful or Faithless?

Faith is confident trust in God and His promises. It is the foundation and starting point in a believer's relationship with God. Our confidence comes from the consistency of God's faithfulness in our lives and to people throughout all of human history. Deuteronomy 7:9 captures this truth: "Know therefore that the Lord your God is God; he is the faithful God, keeping his covenant of love to a thousand generations of those who love him and keep his commandments."

Our assurance as followers comes from the faithfulness of God as Father, Son, and Holy Spirit. Hebrews 11:1 says, "Now faith is the assurance of things hoped for, the conviction of things not seen."

HEBREWS 11:1-40

23

Do I Ever Forget When I Forgive?

Forgiveness is releasing others from the debt of their wrongs even though we may never forget, nor will they. God calls His people to forgive as they have also been forgiven by him. Forgiveness reflects his mercy and grace. Relationships are only reconciled though forgiveness, and at times those relationships are even fully restored leading to peace within a family, neighborhood, work team, or our world. Ephesians 4:32 says, "Be kind to one another, tenderhearted, forgiving one another, as God in Christ forgave you."

MATTHEW 6:14

24

Wisdom as Discernment and Discretion

Wisdom is the ability to apply God's truth rightly in life. It is more than knowledge—it is skillful living aligned with God's ways, gained through reverence for Him while listening to him.

Discernment. Knowing *what* to apply in your life from God's wisdom and truth.

Discretion. Knowing *how* to go about applying that wisdom and truth in your life.

These are two sides to the same coin of obedience in Christlikeness.

The writer of Proverbs says, "The fear of the Lord is the beginning of wisdom, and the knowledge of the Holy One is insight."

PROVERBS 9:10

25

Praying Is My Lifeline to God

Prayer is my communication with God through words spoken, thoughts contemplated, or silent listening.

Prayer is the believer's lifeline to the God of heaven who is listening. Prayers express adoration, confession, thanksgiving, and our requests to God. The Apostle Paul says, "Do not be anxious about anything, but in everything by prayer and supplication with thanksgiving let your requests be made known to God."

PHILIPPIANS 4:6

26

Loving and Being Loved

Love is selfless concern for others and sacrificial action to others. It is the greatest commandment and the essence of God's own personality. It guides what God does in all human relationships. It is our platinum rule as followers of Jesus. The Apostle Paul wrote these words to the church in the city of Corinth: "And now these three remain: faith, hope and love. But the greatest of these is love."

1 CORINTHIANS 13:13

27

JUST Because

Doing justice is the result of God's righteous judgment and fairness according to his holy standards. The Bible emphasizes the connection between God's perfect justice toward us and his call for his people to act justly toward others.

> ...To act justly – Means to live with fairness, integrity, and a commitment to what is right in relationships, decisions, and in society. It reflects the moral order of God's Kingdom.

> ...To love mercy – Calls for compassion, forgiveness, and kindness toward others. It's not merely doing merciful things but loving mercy – making grace a natural response.

> ...To walk humbly with your God – Is about daily dependence, surrender, and intimacy with God, acknowledging his authority and wisdom in every area of life.

Which of these three needs more practice in your life? Micah summarizes true faith in action: "He has shown you...what is good. And what does the Lord require of you but to do justice, and to love kindness, and to walk humbly with your God?"

MICAH 6:8

28

I'm a Manager?

Stewardship begins with an understanding of God's ownership and our responsibility. Everything we have belongs to God, and we are responsible to manage these gifts and resources: our time, talent, and treasure. As followers of Jesus, we manage these areas of our life for God's purposes and his glory. Psalm 24:1 reminds us: "The earth is the Lord's, and everything in it, the world, and all who live in it."

Time. It represents how we invest our days and priorities.

Talent. It represents how we use our gifts and skills for the good of others.

Treasure. It represents how we handle money with integrity and generosity.

Paul reminds us: "Moreover, it is required of stewards that they be found faithful" (1 Corinthians 4:2). Paul reinforces Jesus' teaching about responsibility and accountability: "For everyone who has been given much, much will be required; and from the one who has been entrusted with much, much more will be asked,"

LUKE 12:48

29

Sin, Sinned, Sinning, Sinner

Sin is rebellion against God's will. It addresses what hurts you or what hurts others. God loves us so much, he doesn't want us to hurt ourselves or others. As a result, when we sin, it always separates the sinner from God.

The good news of the Bible the story of God's plan of forgiveness and redemption through Christ. God takes the initiative on our behalf to provide a way to close the gap between the sinner and God. Paul includes all of us in his reality check: "For everyone has sinned; we all fall short of God's glorious standard. Yet God, in his grace, freely makes us right in his sight. He did this through Christ Jesus when he freed us from the penalty for our sins. For God presented Jesus as the sacrifice for sin. People are made right with God when they believe that Jesus sacrificed his life, shedding his blood...he makes sinners right in his sight when they believe in Jesus."

ROMANS 3:23-26

30

I'm Saved from,
and I'm Saved for

God's forgiveness offers deliverance that saves us from sin and its consequences through Christ. Salvation is God's gift of grace, received by faith, saving us for an abundant new life in Christ.

By grace – God's unearned favor meaning salvation is a divine gift, not a human achievement.

Through faith – Faith is the open hand that receives God's gift. It is trust in what Jesus has done rather than what we can do.

Not from yourselves…not by works – Reminds us that no amount of moral effort, good deeds, or religious activity can save us.

So that no one can boast – Our humility recognizes that all credit belongs to God who rescues us purely out of love.

"For by grace you have been saved through faith.
And this is not your own doing; it is the gift of God."

EPHESIANS 2:8

31

Hope for those Hoping

Christian hope is the confident expectation grounded in the character and promises of God. Biblical hope isn't wishful thinking: "I hope it works out." Biblical hope is: "I know God will be faithful fulfilling his promises." Hope steadies us when life feels uncertain, keeping us grounded in God's truth amid the storms of doubt, suffering, or fear.

Hope looks backward – Thanking God for his consistent faithfulness.

Hope looks forward – Trusting God's promises even when life feels uncertain.

Hope looks upward – Finding confidence not in circumstances but in Christ.

Hope looks inward – Renewing our hearts through the Holy Spirit's strength.

The writer of Hebrews clarifies our hope: "We have this hope as an anchor for the soul, firm and secure."

HEBREWS 6:19

JUNE

WHAT A BEAUTIFUL NAME

"Therefore God exalted him to the highest place and gave him the name that is above every name, that at the name of Jesus to the every knee should bow, in heaven and on earth, and every tongue acknowledge that Jesus Christ is Lord, to the glory of God the Father."

— PHILIPPIANS 2:9-11

What a Beautiful Name

You were the Word at the beginning
One with God the Lord Most High
Your hidden glory in creation
Now revealed in you our Christ

you didn't want heaven without us
So Jesus, you brought heaven down
My sin was great, your love was greater
What could separate us now

Death could not hold you
The veil tore before you
You silenced the boast, of sin and grave
The heavens are roaring the praise of your glory
For you are raised to life again

You have no rival
You have no equal
Now and forever, God you reign
Yours is the Kingdom
Yours is the Glory
Yours is the name, above all names

What a powerful name it is
What a powerful name it is
The name of Jesus Christ my King
What a powerful name it is
Nothing can stand against
What a powerful name it is
The name of Jesus

What a powerful name it is
The name of Jesus
What a powerful name it is
The name of Jesus[9]

01

What Is the Pentateuch?

The Old Testament is divided into four sections: Law, History, Wisdom, and Prophets. The first five books of the Old Testament are known as the Pentateuch or Books of Law. Here is an overview of each book:

1. **Genesis** – God's creation, humanity's fall, and the beginnings of God's covenant agreement with the patriarchs of the Old Testament.

2. **Exodus** – God redeems Israel from slavery and establishes his covenant and relationships with them.

3. **Leviticus** – God instructs his people to live in holiness through worship, sacrifice, and obedience.

4. **Numbers** – Israel's wilderness journey shows God's faithfulness amid their rebellion and preparation for entering the promised land.

5. **Deuteronomy** – Moses calls Israel to renew their covenant with God and obey him as they prepare to enter the Promised Land.

The Old Testament law becomes the backdrop of obedience to the Law of Christ for those following Jesus today.

ROMANS 10:4

02

Humility

We know it when we see it: a modest view of oneself in light of God's greatness. Jesus taught about humility, but more importantly, he modeled it in the way he lived and the way he related to others. The Bible calls believers to reject pride and walk in humility, recognizing our ultimate dependence on God as we value others above ourselves. It is a calling to an other-centered life. Humility is never a weakness. It is strength under God's control.

Humble yourselves – It means to willingly submit to God's authority, acknowledging dependence on God rather than on yourself or someone else. It is more of an inward attitude of the heart than just outward modesty.

Before the Lord – It reminds us that humility is not about comparing ourselves to others, but it is about living in honest awareness of God's greatness and our need for his grace.

He will lift you up – God exalts the humble in his time and in his way. The "lifting" may be strength in trials, restoration after failure, or honor that reflects his glory rather than ours.

The brother of Jesus wrote: "Humble yourselves before the Lord, and he will exalt you."

JAMES 4:10

03

Obedience

Obedience is an outward expression of our genuine faith. Obedience reflects our willing submission to God's place in our lives. It is a demonstration of our love for God through how we live and apply God's truth in every relationship, every conversation, and every decision. It's not about earning God's approval. It is an expression of our trust in God. God doesn't demand perfection. He desires priority.

> ...Obedience means **trusting God's wisdom** over our own understanding. Proverbs 3:5-6

> ...Obedience means **choosing God's ways** even when it costs us something. Luke 9:23

> ...Obedience means living in **alignment with God's truth** because we believe God has a heart for our good. Colossians 3:23-24

John reminds us of God's invitation: "If you love me, you will keep my commandments."

JOHN 14:15

04

Grace That's More Than Amazing

Grace is the heartbeat of the Christian story. It is God giving us what we could never earn and don't deserve. God offers it to anyone regardless of what they have done or haven't done.

Grace means that salvation begins and ends with God, not with us.

Grace can only be received as a free gift that God offers and we willingly receive.

Grace doesn't ignore sin. It overcomes sin. It meets us at our worst and calls us into God's best. It frees us from guilt, replaces shame with peace, and transforms obligation into gratitude.

We spend much of our time in life striving to earn approval – from parents, coaches, teachers, bosses, spouses, even from ourselves. Grace interrupts that endless striving. It whispers, "You are loved not because of who you are, but because of who God is."

The church in Corinth needed to be reminded of this good news: "My grace is sufficient for you, for my power is made perfect in weakness."

2 CORINTHIANS 12:9

05

Repentance Repeated

Repentance is one of the most often misunderstood aspects of faith. It is not about guilt or punishment. It is about change and renewal. The Greek word for repentance means a change of mind. To repent means turning 180 degrees in the opposite direction of your thinking and your actions moving you away from sin and toward God. It is a complete turning around of your heart and your purpose for living.

Repentance involves both sorrow for sin and an intentional and willful change of direction. Forgiveness and restoration follow repentance. It's not merely saying, "I'm sorry." It is choosing a new way to live.

Repentance is a decision – It is our response to the Holy Spirit's conviction of conscience.

Repentance is a gift – It is God's invitation to start again.

Repentance brings freedom, not shame. It wipes the slate clean, renews relationship with God, and restores joy that sin always diminishes.

Repentance is not a one-time event. It is a daily posture of your heart, your soul, your mind, and your strength.

This was the message of the early church: "Repent therefore, and turn back, that your sins may be blotted out."

ACTS 3:19

06

Sanctification Is the Daily Process of Becoming More Like Jesus

At first, sanctification is taking baby steps in becoming more like Jesus. The meaning of being holy is the idea that you are set apart for something God has planned just for you.

The Holy Spirit leads us and empowers us to grow in Christlike character and obedience. Early followers of Jesus needed this instruction: "For God's will was for us to be made holy by the sacrifice of the body of Jesus Christ, once for all time" (Hebrews 10:10).

For God's will – It refers to God's divine will and plan for salvation. From eternity, God's purpose was to redeem humanity through his son. Hebrews10:7.

We have been made holy – Holiness is not something we achieve, but something Christ accomplishes for us. Through faith in him, believers are set apart for God.

Through the sacrifice of Christ – Jesus made a physical sacrifice on the cross. His death was not symbolic. He substituted for us, and it was complete. He stepped in and took our place, and his sacrifice was a once for all time sacrifice.

HEBREWS 10:1-10

07

The Peace of God Is Unbelievable

True and lasting peace doesn't come from circumstances but from God himself, regardless of circumstances. Peace is more about connection with God through prayer and trust. When we bring our worries to God, he doesn't always change the situation – but he always changes us within those situations. Peace is both a gift of being right with God, and it is a fruit of the Spirit when we are filled with the Holy Spirit.

The Philippian church was reminded of this while Paul was writing this letter from prison: "And the peace of God, which surpasses all understanding, will guard your hearts and your minds in Christ Jesus" (Philippians 4:7). The Greek word for *guard* is a military term, meaning "to stand watch." God's peace acts like a sentry over our emotions and our thoughts, protecting us from fear and despair.

PHILIPPIANS 4:4-9

08

United in Purpose and Calling

Unity within the local church isn't the absence of conflict but the ability to handle conflict peacefully. It's not the ideal. It is a calling. Unity isn't something we create. It is something we protect because it already exists through the Holy Spirit. Unity is fragile and sacred. It can be fractured by pride, gossip, rumor and resentment. Yet it can be strengthened by humility, gentleness, and patience.

The Ephesian church was learning about this just as we are: "Make every effort to keep the unity of the Spirit through the bond of peace" (Ephesians 4:3).

Make every effort – Unity requires intentionality. Paul calls for diligence, patience, and humility. It doesn't happen by accident. It is maintained by effort and interpersonal grace.

To keep the unity of the Spirit – The Holy Spirit is the source of true unity among believers. He brings people of different backgrounds, temperaments, and opinions into one local church family through shared faith in Christ.

Through the bond of peace – Peace is the glue that holds unity together. It's not the absence of disagreement, but the presence of Christlike love that prioritizes reconciliation over division. Read Ephesians 4:4-6 to learn about oneness that God models and makes possible.

EPHESIANS 4:3-6

09

Self-Serving or Other-Serving?

Service within the Christian community focuses on meeting the needs of others first in a spirit of love. Jesus demonstrated what leadership is all about with a towel not a throne. He defined greatness by kneeling to wash the feet of his disciples. He touched the untouchable in his healing ministry. He died for those who least deserved it.

Jesus' example calls us to live with the same attitude of being other-centered – to serve, give, and love without expectation of reward. To follow Jesus is to live for others instead of above others.

Service flows from humility and gratitude to God, following the example of Jesus who came to serve, never to be served. Mark recorded it: "For even the Son of Man came not to be served but to serve, and to give his life as a ransom for many."

MARK 10:45

10

Temptation

Our world offers a multitude of distractions from holy living. There are daily temptations to disobey God.

While temptation itself is not sin, the Bible tells us that giving into it is sin. God always promises to provide the strength we will need in those moments, and he provides a way to escape from those temptations.

The city of Corinth had temptations on every block, so Paul reminds the followers of Jesus: "No temptation has overtaken you that is not common to man. God is faithful... with the temptation he will also provide the way of escape" (1 Corinthians 10:13).

This verse is both a warning and a promise. It is a reminder of human weakness and God's faithfulness. Temptation is a universal experience. God doesn't remove temptation but never abandons us in it. He knows your limits and sets boundaries around every test or trial. The way out is more often endurance than escape. God provides the strength, wisdom, and courage to resist sin and remain faithful.

1 CORINTHIANS 10:12-14

11

Where Could You Live Forever?

God's promise of eternity is unending life in God's presence through Christ. Eternal life actually begins now in your relationship with Jesus and then that relationship continues forever in God's presence after Christ's second coming.

"He has made everything beautiful in its time. He has also set eternity in the human heart; yet no one can fathom what God has done from beginning to end" (Ecclesiastes 3:11). Solomon reminds us that eternity is a quiet longing in every human heart. It is the sense that we were made for something more than time can contain. We live now, but we were created for eternity.

> ...Eternity is a reminder that this world is temporary, but God's Kingdom is eternal. That gives a different perspective to whatever happens to us in this world. It offers hope beyond our last breath.

> ...Jesus wasn't talking so much about endless time. He was describing an endless relationship. Eternal life begins the moment we believe in Christ and continues uninterrupted into forever.

ECCLESIASTES 3:9-11

12

What Is the History of Ancient Israel?

Twelve books of history follow the first five books in the Old Testament and tell the historical story that is carefully preparing for God's coming Messiah:

Joshua – Israel mostly conquers and settles the Promised Land under Joshua's leadership.

Judges – Israel goes through repeated cycles of sin, oppression, deliverance, and failure.

Ruth – God's providence and loyalty are shown through Ruth's faithfulness and David's family line.

1 Samuel – Israel transitions from judges to kings with the rise of Samuel, Saul, and David.

2 Samuel – David's reign brings triumphs and failures, showing God's covenant faithfulness.

1 Kings – Solomon's reign and the kingdom's division reveal both glory and decline.

2 Kings – The divided kingdoms fall into sin, leading to exile in Assyria and Babylon.

1 Chronicles – David's reign highlights worship in the temple and living by God's covenant promises.

2 Chronicles – This book is defined by a record of the kings of Judah, temple worship, and the consequences of unfaithfulness.

Ezra – Israel returns from exile and begins to rebuild the temple and restore worship.

Nehemiah – Nehemiah leads in rebuilding Jerusalem's walls and renewing their covenant faithfulness with God.

Esther – God preserves his people through Esther's courage, even in exile.

The Old Testament is a continuing story of how God works in the lives of people just like you and me. God is still the same faithful, forgiving God who calls us to holy living and obedience that we read of throughout the history of Israel.

PSALM 105:5

13

There Was a Beginning to All That Is

Creation is God's act of bringing the universe into existence. The first words of Scripture remind us of how it all started: "In the beginning, God created the heavens and the earth."

...The book of Genesis is clear about "what" happened at the beginning.

...Science helps us understand "how" the universe began and developed.

...Faith explains "who" created it all and "why."

Each speaks to different dimensions of the same reality. They are complementary, not competing truths.

GENESIS 1

14

Our Agreement with God

In Bible times, covenants were a common part of diplomacy among the political powers of the day. They were formal agreements – often sealed with vows, rituals, witnesses, and at times sacrifices that confirmed mutual obligations. Covenants were used to establish peace, military alliances, trade agreements, and mutual protection.

"Covenant" in the Old Testament was a binding agreement initiated by God with his chosen people. The covenant stories reveal God's commitment and faithfulness. We see that in the covenants God made with Noah, Abraham, and Israel. The old leads to the new in the coming of Christ. In the New Covenant, Jesus replaces the earlier covenant for all believers today, and we see the same commitment and faithfulness of God in his work of redemption through Christ's death and resurrection.

God's Covenant with Abraham: "I will establish my covenant between me and you and your offspring after you."

GENESIS 17:7

15

Laws for Ancient Israel

The Old Testament law is recorded in the first five books of the Old Testament, The Pentateuch. It represents God's commands given to guide and protect the Hebrew people on their journey to become the nation of Israel. God blessed this group of nomads who became a great nation for one reason: To be a blessing to the whole world not just to be blessed by God themselves.

Israel was entrusted with the revelation of the one true, holy, and covenant-keeping God in a world of idolatry. Israel's worship, ethics, and understanding of God became a light to the nations. "I will also make you a light for the Gentiles, that my salvation may reach to the ends of the earth" (Isaiah 49:6).

"All peoples on earth will be blessed through you."

GENESIS 12:3; 22:18

16

When You Can See
Around the Corner

Prophecy is God's revealed message about his will in the present in light of future events. Prophets called people back to obedience and often pointed toward coming events and the coming Messiah as motivation for obedience today.

The New Testament reflects in this way: "For no prophecy was ever produced by the will of man, but men spoke from God as they were carried along by the Holy Spirit."

The book of Revelation in the New Testament is the culmination of biblical prophecy given to John in his writing a book that closes the Bible's record. John includes prophecies for today's reader that deal with the church, spiritual warfare, the return of Christ, final judgment, and the new creation. The book ends with a warning not to add or take away from the truth contained within (Revelation 22:18-19).

2 PETER 1:21

17

What Do You Pay the Most Attention to?

Idolatry is worshiping anything other than the one, true God. The first of the Ten Commandments, Exodus 20:1-17, says: "You shall have no other gods before me."

It is easy in a complex and busy world to let immediate and urgent issues of work, parenting, commuting, financial or physical challenges, and the uncertainty of life itself get in the way of the more important need to keep God's place in your life in a proper perspective. It's not that God replaces or ignores the rest of your list. Just keep God as number one on your list.

The Bible condemns idols—whether physical or virtual in one's heart—because they replace our devotion to God. When the Apostle Paul visited the city of Athens, he saw their idols to every god they could think of. One idol was ascribed "to an unknown god" just so they didn't miss any gods and then face the consequences of offending that god.

Paul took the opportunity to say: "This God, whom you worship without knowing, is the one I'm telling you about" (Acts 17:23). He told them about the most-high God who was the Creator of the world. Read his words spoken to the Athenians in Acts 17:24-31. Then keep God number one.

ACTS 17:16-34

18

It's God's Kingdom

Jesus' teaching regularly announced the arrival of the Kingdom of God. It is God's reign over everything, present and future. Most importantly it is God's reign as King in the human heart of every living being.

Jesus preached the kingdom as both a present reality in believers' lives and a future fulfillment for all of eternity. The theologians' concept of "the already and not yet" reminds followers of Jesus that they experience the truth of God's Kingdom now through faith, obedience, and the work of the Holy Spirit, while also waiting for its final reality in the age to come. And so, we pray, "Even so, Lord Jesus, come quickly"

MATTHEW 6:33

19

Parenting 401:
Training for a Lifetime

Solomon is credited with the wisdom in Proverbs 22:6: "Train up a child in the way he should go; even when he is old, he will not depart from it." *Training down* implies a reactive way of responding to your child through negative messages that demean and embarrass them in pubic. *Training up* is a developmental way of responding that invites and inspires the child to learn positive habits of how life is to be lived.

Train up implies intentional, formative shaping. The Hebrew word suggests the ideas of dedication, initiation, or narrowing a path. This is not passive parenting. It suggests:

- Consistent modeling, not just instruction.
- Repeated habits, not one-time talks.
- Shaping life values and instincts, not merely modifying their behavior when you are watching.

In the way he should go literally means "according to his or her way." It implies:

- Paying attention to a child's innate temperament, strengths, and wiring.
- Guiding them toward personal growth and development consistent with who they are, not who you want them to be.
- Avoiding one-size-fits-all parenting so you parent each child uniquely.

Will not depart offers a word of hope. What a child learns early often comes back to guide them later on.

- Early formation creates lifelong inner values that guide decisions.
- What is internalized early becomes a compass, even when resisted along the way.
- Solomon's wisdom challenges both extremes: (1) Control-based parenting: forcing compliance without heart formation, and (2) Hands-off parenting: assuming children will "figure it out."

1 CORINTHIANS 3:6

20

Kings and Queens Have Crowns. Why Not You?

Steadfast endurance in faith despite trials is the perseverance of people who follow Jesus. The Christian life often
involves challenges in life, but perseverance proves the
genuineness of your faith and leads to an eternal reward.
The brother of Jesus, James, tells the whole story: "Blessed
is the one who perseveres under trial because, having
stood the test, that person will receive the crown of life."

In the New Testament, the Crown of Life is a metaphor for
the reward of eternal life that God gives to believers who
remain faithful to him, especially to those who persevere
through trials, suffering, and temptation.

JAMES 1:12

21

Death Is an Enemy, But...

Resurrection means being raised from death to new life just like Lazarus. Just like Jesus. Just like you. Christ's resurrection is the foundation of Christian hope as believers look forward to their own resurrection to eternal life. The resurrection of Jesus confirms that he is the Son of God, proves his sacrifice for sin was accepted, guarantees believers' resurrection, and gives hope beyond death.

The resurrection was historical – Jesus physically rose from the dead on the third day (Matthew 28, Luke 24, and John 20-21).

The resurrection was supernatural – God's power over death raised Jesus from the grave (Acts 2:24; Romans 6:4).

The resurrection was transformational – Jesus rose with a glorified, immortal body (1 Corinthians 15:20-23).

Jesus promised it: "I am the resurrection and the life. The one who believes in me will live, even though they die."

JOHN 11:25

22

I'll Be Back

The Second Coming refers to the future return of Jesus Christ. Scripture promises that Jesus will come again to judge the world and fully establish God's kingdom. No one knows the day or the hour. Jesus didn't. The angels didn't. We don't. We are invited to live every day in light of what is coming regardless of how long it takes.

Paul looks forward to what we do know: "For the Lord himself will descend from heaven with a cry of command... and the dead in Christ will rise first."

1 THESSALONIANS 4:16

23

How Much Wisdom Is There in the Wisdom Books of the Old Testament?

Five books make up the wisdom literature that follows the first five books of law and the twelve books of history in the Old Testament record of ancient Israel. There was truth in these wisdom writings for the original listeners, and there is truth for us today.

Job – Explores suffering, faith, and God's sovereignty through Job's trials and perseverance.

Psalms – A collection of prayers, songs, and worship poetry expressing the full range of human emotion toward God.

Proverbs – Practical wisdom for living a godly life that is grounded in awe and reverence for the Lord.

Ecclesiastes – Reflects on the futility of life apart from God and the meaning found only in him.

Song of Solomon (Song of Songs) – Celebrates love, marriage, and the beauty of covenant intimacy.

24

Is This All Really True?

Truth always aligns with God's character and his spoken word. His faithful consistency through all generations is a validation of the truth of God's very character! The Bible reminds us that God is Truth, His Word is Truth, and Christ is the embodiment of Truth. If not God, what is your standard of what is true and good to guide you ethically and justly through life?

John records these words: "Sanctify them in the truth; your word is truth."

JOHN 17:17

25

Mercy in Action

God's mercy is **sympathy** and **empathy** in action toward the undeserving. Mercy is the passive expression of your sympathy and then the active expression of your empathy.

The First Step. Sympathy is feeling **for** someone. It's all in your head.

The Second Step. Empathy is acting **with** someone. It's all in your heart.

The first step is easier. Some people only take that step.

God demonstrates mercy by withholding punishment and offering forgiveness. He takes both steps in our lives. He feels for us and he acts on our behalf.

- Do you show mercy in your **attitudes** toward others?

- Do you show mercy in your **words** toward others?

- Do you show mercy in your **actions** toward others?

The Beatitudes listed in Matthew 5 are blessings. To be blessed means to be spiritually favored, approved by God, and full of joy – not because of circumstances, but because of living a life in alignment with God's character. Jesus' Beatitudes includes the call to be full of mercy: "Blessed are the merciful, for they shall receive mercy."

MATTHEW 5:7

26

Wait Well, Live Well

Patience under fire is when followers of Jesus endure hardship or deal with unexpected waiting without frustration or complaint. Patience is one of the fruits of the Holy Spirit reflecting God's own long-suffering toward humanity.

Peter uses God as an example for us: "The Lord is not slow to fulfill his promise… but is patient toward you." In traffic or in a long line at the grocery store today, use the delay to reflect on how patient God is with you.

2 PETER 3:9

27

Generosity Changes Both the Receiver and the Giver

Generosity is a willingness to give freely of your time, skills, resources, and love.

We pay it forward because of God's generosity with us out of his self-giving nature.

The Corinthian church was learning generosity: "Each one must give as he has decided in his heart, not reluctantly or under compulsion, for God loves a cheerful giver."

2 CORINTHIANS 9:7

28

Joy Doesn't Wait for Perfect

Joy differs from happiness. Joy is a deep-seated perspective on life rooted in God, not the rollercoaster of our circumstances.

Joy is the mark of a believers' character because of their trust in God's promises and God's presence in their life, even during the trials of daily life.

Being joyful is a way to bring light and salt to those around you (Matthew 5:13-16). Joy is noticed by others because it is so rare. When people wonder how you can keep smiling, tell them about the difference Jesus makes.

The church in the city of Philippi needed Paul's reminder: "Rejoice in the Lord always; again, I will say, rejoice."

PHILIPPIANS 4:4

29

Holy Spirit Inside,
Holy Living Outside

When Jesus was leaving for Heaven, after his resurrection, he promised his followers that he would send the Holy Spirit to live within them, even as he had been living with them. Paul describes our bodies as dwelling places of the Holy Spirit and says as a result, our bodies are called a holy temple.

Paul's point is a reminder of a promise that God's presence now resides in his people. When that is true, it means we take God with us wherever we go. It changes every part of every day. It changes every interaction with others. It changes how we take care of our "temple." It changes the way we live. It changes the impact we have on others around us.

Remind yourself each new day what Paul said to the followers of Jesus in the city of Corinth: "Do you not know that your body is a temple of the Holy Spirit within you...?"

1 CORINTHIANS 6:19

30

Healing Is the Art of Becoming Whole Again

Healing is the restoration of physical, emotional, or spiritual wholeness. God is revealed as healer in both Old and New Testaments. Ultimate spiritual healing is found in Christ.

Many of the scars we carry in this life will see eternal healing in Heaven. The Apostle Paul prayed three times for release from his "thorn in the flesh." God's answer: "My grace is sufficient for you. My power is made perfect in weakness." And Paul's reply: "Therefore I am content with weaknesses, with insults, with troubles, with persecutions and difficulties for the sake of Christ, for whenever I am, then I am strong" (2 Corinthians 12: 8-9).

The writer of Psalms adds this encouragement, "He heals the brokenhearted and binds up their wounds."

PSALM 147:3

JULY

THE
PRAYER

"The Lord is near to all who call on Him, to all who call on Him in truth."

— PSALM 145:18

The Prayer

I pray you'll be our eyes
And watch us where we go
And help us to be wise
In times when we don't know

Let this be our prayer
When we lose our way
Lead us to a place
Guide us with your grace
To a place where we'll be safe.

I pray we'll find your light
And hold it in our hearts

When stars go out each night
Remind us where you are.

When shadows fill our day
Lead us to a place

Guide us with your grace
To a place where we'll be safe.
And watch us from above

Just like every child.
Needs to find a place
Guide us with your grace.
Give us faith so we'll be safe[10]

01

Rest Is Resistance to Hurry

God's rhythm of resting one day in seven is to give us time for renewal of body, mind, and spirit through fellowship with God. Rest is modeled in creation, commanded in the Sabbath, and fulfilled in Christ's promise of ultimate and eternal restoration. Jesus timely and timeless offer: "Come to me, all who labor and are heavy laden, and I will give you rest" (Matthew 11:28).

When you follow God's example, what's your rhythm of resting and restoration?

- Which day is your seventh day of the week?
- How do you practice Sabbath rest?
- What is most important for you on this one day in seven?
- Does your practice contribute to your spiritual restoration?
- What most often interrupts this day for you or your family?

Rest is more than recreation. It is re-creation of who God made you to be and what he called you to do.

MATTHEW 11:28-30

02

Light Always
Overcomes Darkness

Light is a symbol of truth, purity, and God's presence. The Bible contrasts light with darkness, calling believers to walk in God's light.

There are always dark days in our lives and in our world. We may wonder what happened to God. Where is he? Why isn't he at work on my behalf? God's promises light even when we may not see anything hopeful: "The light shines in darkness, and the darkness has not overcome it" (John 1:5).

When we walk in his light we also shine more brightly. Never turn off God's light or yours! Jesus said it: "I am the light of the world. Whoever follows me will not walk in darkness but will have the light of life."

JOHN 8:12

03

What Did the Major Prophets in the Old Testament See Coming in the Future?

Five books of prophecy by the "Major Prophets" follow the Wisdom literature of the Old Testament. They are looking around an obscure corner seeing a new day that others could not yet see because of their current circumstances. They were living in exile. The prophets were announcing hope for hopeless people once they turned back to God in obedience.

Isaiah – Calls God's people in Judah to repentance, warns of judgment, and foretells the coming Messiah and God's salvation.

Jeremiah – Proclaims God's judgment on Judah for their unfaithfulness, yet he promises a new covenant of hope.

Lamentations – Laments and mourns Jerusalem's destruction, yet the writer affirms God's mercy and faithfulness.

Ezekiel – Uses visions and symbolic acts to warn of judgment and reveal God's plan to restore his people.

Daniel – Shows God's sovereignty through Daniel's faithfulness in exile and visions of future kingdoms.

DEUTERONOMY 18:18

04

Every Day Is
Independence Day

Each year on July 4th Americans celebrate Independence Day to commemorate the signing of the Declaration of Independence in 1776. This is an annual reminder of those who sacrificed for the freedoms we enjoy: Freedom of speech, worship, and opportunity. It is a reminder that freedom is precious and never free.

The Apostle Paul reminds us of our spiritual freedom in Christ. Jesus offers us a deeper and eternal freedom. It's freedom from sin, guilt, fear, and death. Paul reminds us that appreciation for our freedom motivates us to an other-focused life: "You, my brothers and sisters, were called to be free. But do not use your freedom to indulge the flesh; rather serve one another humbly in love."

GALATIANS 5:13

05

Great Is Thy Faithfulness

Faithfulness implies steadfast loyalty and continuing reliability. God's faithfulness is the foundation of our trust in him. Even in seasons of mourning, God's promise always shines through: "The steadfast love of the Lord never ceases; his mercies never come to an end; they are new every morning; great is your faithfulness" (Lamentations 3:23-24).

Believers are called to reflect that faithful quality in all relationships and in every commitment made to others. Our word is to be our truth.

- Can people count on you?
- Do you under-promise and over-deliver?
- Do you even promise?

How do you respond to those who promise you but don't follow through?

LAMENTATIONS 1:1-5:22

06

Your Story Is His Witness

Witnesses testify of their experience every day in court rooms around the world. As follower of Jesus, we are called to be witnesses of what God has done in our life. When it's your personal story, others can't deny it.

We bear witness to Christ in both the words we speak and in the life we live. When we earn the right to be heard by others, we have the opportunity to point them to Jesus. It's what Jesus commanded followers to do at the end of his earthly ministry, "Go and make disciples of all nations" (Matthew 28:19).

Luke reminds the early church of a promise and a calling that follows. Your witness always starts at home but doesn't stop there: "But you will receive power when the Holy Spirit has come upon you, and you will be my witnesses in Jerusalem, and in all Judea, and Samaria, and to the ends of the earth."

ACTS 1:8

07

Persecution Never Stops Faith. It Always Spreads Faith

Persecution was hostility faced by followers of Jesus in the first century because of their faith in Christ. The Bible prepares believers for opposition, encouraging endurance and trust in God's final justice.

Even today followers of Jesus are being persecuted globally when they are silenced, are canceled, are marginalized, are assumed less than, or even are martyred for what they believe. Keep speaking anyway. When you know it's right, never compromise.

Paul advised the younger Timothy: "Indeed, all who desire to live a godly life in Christ Jesus will be persecuted."

2 TIMOTHY 3:12

08

Blessing Is God's Fingerprint on Your Life

To be blessed is evidence of God's favor and goodness freely given to you. Blessings may be spiritual or material. They are ultimately meant to glorify God in our lives and then paid forward to the benefit of others.

When God chose the Hebrews to be his people, it wasn't to play favorites. They were "blessed to be a blessing" to the world. See Genesis 12:2-3.

This is how God taught Moses and Aaron to bless the Israelites: "The Lord bless you and keep you; the Lord make his face to shine upon you..." That blessing continues in our lives today. When God makes his face to shine on you, then consider how you can pay it forward to a child, a spouse, a neighbor, a co-worker, even an enemy.

NUMBERS 6:24-25

09

God's Anger Appeased, God's Love Unleashed

The theological term *propitiation* means the ending of God's judgment through sacrifice. In the New Testament, Christ's death is described as the once-for-all sacrifice that satisfies God's justice in light of our sin that separates us from God.

In one of John's three short books at the end of the New Testament, he includes this declaration: "He is the propitiation for our sins, and not for ours only but also for the sins of the whole world" (1 John 2:2). That is good news. God is not angry with us even when we sin. He loves us too much to leave us separated in our relationship with him. Jesus is our *propitiation*. "While we were yet sinners, Christ died for us."

ROMANS 5:8

10

Holiness Is Wholeness in God

Something holy is something set apart for a special purpose. Spiritually speaking, holiness means being set apart for God's purpose in your life. Holiness is God's very nature, and it is our calling to seek and live holiness in daily living.

When we choose to follow Jesus, our life is set apart for something God had planned before we were even born (Psalm 139:16). Then, throughout our lives, God orders our steps (Psalm 37:23). Thank God for the holiness he has given you. Then follow his lead. Let tomorrow take care of itself. Don't worry. God will meet you tomorrow for tomorrow's purpose.

God is holy. Jesus is holy. The Spirit is holy. And so, you are called to be holy: "You shall be holy, for I the Lord your God am holy."

LEVITICUS 19:2

11

Redemption Is Rescue with a Purpose

Redemption is deliverance for personal freedom made possible by someone paying the price that is due. Paying a bond does it temporarily in our court system. When God redeems us from sin, he is paying the price due in full forever.

The Bible uses the imagery of our slavery to sin. It implies living in exile from God because sin separates us from fellowship with God. What is due for your sin was paid in full through Christ's sacrifice on the cross.

The church in Ephesus was reminded of this in Paul's letter sent to them: "In him we have redemption through his blood, the forgiveness of sins, in accordance with the riches of God's grace."

EPHESIANS 1:7

12

God's Glory Is His Signature on Creation

Glory is a word used to describe the majesty and splendor of God. Glory belongs to God alone. The conclusion at the end of the Lord's Prayer is: "Thine is the Kingdom and the power and the glory forever." We can honestly pray what the Lord's Prayer addresses (provision, pardon, and protection) when we acknowledge that following Jesus is about building his Kingdom (not ours), in his power (not our best efforts), and for his glory (not to make us look good). God gets all the glory!

Life in the city of ancient Corinth gave every opportunity to glory in everything except God. So, Paul recalibrates their thinking in everything they do: "So, whether you eat or drink, or whatever you do, do all to the glory of God."

1 CORINTHIANS 10:31

13

Awe and Reverence Leads to Obedience

When the Bible says to "fear God" it's not about being afraid of a tyrant God as was often true of ancient people who worshipped idols they feared. They were afraid of displeasing their gods and reaping the consequences in their health, safety, or their crops for food. Fear of our God is nothing like the ancients and their array of gods. We worship one God with reverent awe and respect. That kind of biblical fear is the beginning of godly wisdom leading to obedience, humility, and worship of the one true God.

The Proverbs capture the essence of what this means in our lives of following Jesus: "The fear of the Lord is the beginning of knowledge; fools despise wisdom and instruction." Don't be foolish!

PROVERBS 1:7

14

Mission Starts Wherever You Are

The New Testament has a missional vision of sending God's people to share the Jesus' story with others. It doesn't mean we are all supposed to go somewhere far away from home. Some are called and gifted for that. For most of us, it is being on mission right where we are.

The Great Commission of Jesus tells us to "go." Going starts in our own neighborhood or network of personal and professional relationships. Individually we are on mission at home, at school, at work, or anywhere in the community where we live, play, shop, go to school, or work.

The spread of the church globally also fulfills those words of Jesus. Participating in a local church is a collective way to be on mission together serving the world through your church's financial support of global missions in underserved areas of the world.

Other-focused churches understand that the church was never to be a refuge of safety that completely occupies our time keeping us out of the world. The church is always to be on mission no matter how challenging that might be.

The Great Commission: "Go therefore and make disciples of all nations..."

MATTHEW 28:19

15

The Old Testament Closes with 12 Final Prophetic Words

The Minor Prophets add to our understanding of the current condition of the nation of ancient Israel still in exile. The prophets declared what their future could be if they turned back to God in obedience.

Hosea – God's faithful love, in spite of Israel's unfaithfulness, is illustrated through Hosea's marriage.

Joel – Warns of the "Day of the Lord" and promises God's Spirit poured out on his people.

Amos – Condemns social injustice and calls for true righteousness among God's people.

Obadiah – Pronounces judgment on Edom and promises Israel's restoration.

Jonah – Extends God's mercy to all nations, shown through Jonah's reluctant mission to Nineveh.

Micah – Calls for justice, mercy, and humility while promising a coming ruler from the little town of Bethlehem.

Nahum – Declares God's judgment on Nineveh for its cruelty and sin.

Habakkuk – Wrestles with God's justice but affirms that the righteous live by faith.

Zephaniah – Warns of the coming "Day of the Lord" and promises future restoration.

Haggai – Urges the people to rebuild the temple and put God first.

Zechariah – Encourages the returned exiles with visions of restoration and the coming Messiah.

Malachi – Confronts spiritual apathy and promises the coming of the God's messianic messenger.

AMOS 3:7

16

Do It Afraid, Do It Anyway

Courage is boldness and strength in the face of fear or danger. The Bible often calls God's people to have courage rooted not in themselves, but in God's presence and God's promises. Jesus' final words to his followers included these: "And surely I am with you always, to the very end of the age" (Matthew 28:20).

Courage comes from the Latin word meaning "heart." At its core, it means having the inner strength of heart to face fear, danger, difficulty, or uncertainty with great resolve. God will do his part when we do our part. Where do you need courage (heart) today?

In the Old Testament, God was leading his people to their promised land. They stood at the edge of the Jordan River anticipating the enemies on the other side. God promised that his part in the victory was to be with Joshua in leading the nation forward, and so he said in Joshua 1:9, "Be strong and courageous."

Joshua also had a role to play alongside what God promised. God challenged Joshua: "Keep this Book of the Law always on your lips; meditate on it day and night, so that you may be careful to do everything written it. Then you will be prosperous and successful."

JOSHUA 1:8

17

In Suffering, Hope Anchors the Soul

Hope is an unshakable confidence in God's promises to see us through hardship. Suffering is never easy. It costs more than we want to pay, but there is a payback.

Suffering is never without meaning for believers. Paul's writing on this topic doesn't suggest that we enjoy the pain, but he recognizes that God can use suffering for our good. God doesn't cause suffering but allows it as the consequence of living in a broken and fallen world.

In this in-between time from Christ's first coming to his second coming, we will have trials and tribulations. In writing to the Corinthian church, Paul says, "We are hard pressed on every side, but not crushed; perplexed, but not in despair" (2 Corinthians 4:8).

How can we have that unshakable confidence and see God bring good out of our suffering? Paul was able to say in his own suffering: "We rejoice in our sufferings, knowing that suffering produces endurance, and endurance produces character, and character produces hope."

ROMANS 5:3-4

18

Hospitality Is Love
with Open Doors

Some are given the spiritual gift of hospitality by welcoming and caring for others, especially strangers as if they were family. The Latin origin of the word hospitality means "friendliness to guests." No wonder the word includes "hospital." That is hospitality in the deepest, most physical sense.

Hospitality reflects God's generous welcome to us, and it was a mark of early Christian communities. Churches can collectively be hospitals for spiritually depleted people. That requires a welcoming environment when first-timers step through the door of a church. Perhaps it is the toughest moment for anyone far from God. They are not sure what to expect and if it will be possible to exit if things get awkward.

The early church grew because of their gracious hospitality. Their house rule was non-negotiable: "Do not neglect to show hospitality to strangers, for thereby some have entertained angels unawares." How hospitable are you?

HEBREWS 13:2

19

Discipline Is the Bridge from Knowing to Doing to Becoming

Discipline is the experience of training and correction that leads to maturity. It has the same root meaning as "disciple." The core idea is of someone who is a continuing learner. Essentially, discipline means structured learning with application, and the kind of training that shapes character and behavior. It is the consistent practice of new habits that shapes the excellence of any athlete or performer.

God uses disciplines to shape believers into Christlikeness. It's learning from life experiences, good and bad, to develop new habits of how we respond and how we train further for increasing spiritual maturity. Sometimes discipline is correction as in Hebrews 12:6. At other times is it training for godliness as in 1 Timothy 4:7.

The writer captures the essence of discipline for the purpose of correction: "For the Lord disciplines the one he loves..."

HEBREWS 12:6

20

Contentment Is Saying: "It's Enough"

When you are at peace and have an inner satisfaction that doesn't depend on better circumstances with more possessions, that is contentment. Unlike complacency, contentment is an active trust in God's provision.

Timothy suggests that true wealth isn't measured in possessions but in peace: "Godliness with contentment is great gain." (1 Timothy 6:6). If you earn more and then you can get more, are you happier? Are you more or less at peace?

Paul learned that contentment comes with trusting God's provision rather than continually chasing more: "I have learned in whatever situation I am to be content."

PHILIPPIANS 4:11

21

Faith Makes Us Righteous. Obedience Makes It Visible.

Righteousness is conformity to God's standards of holiness. It leads to living in a right relationship with God and living right interpersonally.

Righteousness is both a gift we receive from God through Christ and then a behavior we live out in daily life.

Jesus taught us the how to do that: "But seek first the kingdom of God and his righteousness, and all these things will be added to you."

MATTHEW 6:33

22

Friends Are the Family We Choose

Friendship is a mutual bond of trust, loyalty, and mutual support. The word "friend" comes from an Old English root word meaning "to love" or "to favor."

Friendship is both a gift from God and a reflection of God's own love for us. The Bible values faithful friendships as a source of reciprocal encouragement, accountability, and strength. Who are your three besties?

- Would they say that about you?
- When is the last time you could have and should have called one of them but did not?
- Why not?

Friends are friends in the best of times and in the worst of times. The book of Proverbs records this wisdom: "A friend loves at all times, and a brother is born for adversity."

PROVERBS 17:17

23

Freedom Is Becoming Who You Were Made to Be

Freedom is what you are *free from*: Christ frees you from the power of sin through forgiveness in every part of your life. Freedom is also what you are *free for*: It's not a license to sin but the ability for right living in service to others.

Freedom is God's gift of becoming who he created you to be!

Those at the church in Galatia were reminded of that truth perhaps for the first time in their lives: "For freedom Christ has set us free; stand firm therefore, and do not submit again to a yoke of slavery."

GALATIANS 5:1

24

Prayer Is Faith Refusing to Quit

Perseverance is persistent, ongoing communication with God. The Bible calls believers to pray continually, trusting that God hears and answers in his timing.

Prayer changes us more than it might change our circumstances. The time we spend waiting for God to answer teaches humility, patience, and trust in God's timing.

The followers of Jesus in the city of Thessalonica needed to hear three words: "Pray without ceasing."

1 THESSALONIANS 5:17

25

Blessed by the Beatitudes

Jesus' Beatitudes turn worldly values upside down, describing the character of kingdom-minded Jesus followers. These are not steps to earn God's favor. Each Beatitude contains a present condition and a future promise.

Poor in spirit - rich in heaven.

Those who mourn will be comforted.

Meekness inherits what pride cannot.

Hungry for righteousness? God will fill.

Mercy received, mercy given.

Pure hearts see God.

Peacemakers carry God's family name.

Persecuted but not forsaken—the kingdom is theirs.

MATTHEW 5:3-12

26

Why Are There Four Accounts of the Gospel Story in the New Testament?

Matthew – Presents Jesus as the promised Messiah and King, fulfilling Old Testament prophecy.

Mark – Emphasizes Jesus as the suffering Servant and Son of God through action-packed accounts.

Luke – Highlights Jesus as the Savior for all people, with a focus on compassion, prayer, and the marginalized.

John – Declares Jesus as the divine Son of God who brings eternal life through belief in Him.

LUKE 1:3-4

27

Whose Acts Are Recorded in Acts?

The New Testament book of Acts records the birth and growth of the early church through the Holy Spirit's power, spreading the Gospel from Jerusalem to the whole world. What could the church today learn from its earliest beginnings in the first century?

What about the Holy Spirit in Acts 2?

What about the primary and sole focus of their message in Acts 2:36?

What about the priority of prayer in Acts 1:14; 4:31; 13:2-3?

What about the quality of their experience of community in Acts 2:42-47

What about their courage in the face of opposition in Acts 5:29?

What about their cross-cultural mission in Acts 10 and 15?

ACTS 2:42-47

28

Coincidence Is Just Providence in Disguise

The word *providence* gets at the ideas of foreseeing and providing. God's providence refers to his active involvement, sovereign care, and continual guidance over creation. Nothing happens by chance!

Sometimes God is working in ways we don't yet see or understand. He always works all things together for his purposes and glory, in spite of the twists and turns of our decisions. Unlike fate or coincidence, providence means that life is intentionally directed by a personal, loving God. Nothing is random in God's world.

Hebrews says, "He upholds the universe by the word of his power.

HEBREWS 1:3

29

Repaying Evil with Good

Paul closes the book of Romans with a powerful principle for Christian living. Evil exists in the world and often people with evil intentions affect our lives.

- The typical human response is retaliation to repay wrong for wrong.

- Paul says the way of Christ is different. We conquer evil, not by mirroring it, but by doing good in return.

Evil never ends when we respond to evil with more of the same. Responding to wrongs with kindness and righteousness breaks the cycle of revenge and opens the door for reconciliation. When we return good for evil, we reflect Christ's mercy by overcoming evil through love.

Here are Paul's final thoughts at the end of Romans: "Do not be overcome by evil but overcome evil with good."

ROMANS 12:21

30

Confession Empties the Heart
So Grace Can Fill it Up

Confession is agreement with God. Our confession of sin is not new information for God. He already knows everything about us. It is our honesty in acknowledging our sins before God (confession) that leads to forgiveness, cleansing, and restored fellowship with God.

Confession doesn't just clear up our past record, it reorients how we live in the future. When we are silent about our sin, it strengthens its control on our life. When we speak the truth to God in confession, it exposes sin to the light and therefore loses its power. Then our relationship with God is restored, and God's grace is renewed within us!

The joy of forgiveness starts when this is true: "If we confess our sins, he is faithful and just to forgive us our sins..."

1 JOHN 1:9

31

Discernment

What: The ability to distinguish truth from error.
(John 8:31-32)

So What: Believers are called to test everything by God's
Word and Spirit to avoid deception. (1 John 4:1)

Now What: "Are you testing everything and hold on to
what is good." (1 Thessalonians 5:21)

PROVERBS 15:14

AUGUST

THE
BLESSING

*"Praise be to the God and Father of our
Lord Jesus Christ, who has blessed us in
the heavenly realms with every spiritual
blessing in Christ."*

— EPHESIANS 1:3

The Blessing

The Lord bless you
And keep you
Make his face shine upon you
And be gracious to you
The Lord turn his
Face toward you
And give you peace

May his favor be upon you
And a thousand generations
And your family and your children
And their children, and their children

May his presence go before you
And behind you, and beside you
All around you, and within you
He is with you, he is with you

In the morning, in the evening
In your coming, and your going
In your weeping, and rejoicing
He is for you, he is for you[11]

01

Steadfast Faith Stands Regardless

Steadfast in faith means to remain, to endure, or to stand firm under trials. James 1:2 says, "Blessed is the one who remains steadfast under trial…" It's not passive waiting for heaven; it's active endurance that lives with the hope of a better day ahead.

God is described as having a steadfast love. Psalm 136 repeats the word 26 times as it refers to God. Our steadiness flows from God's steadiness. He never quits on us, so we can't quit on him.

The Apostle Paul ends his first letter to the church in the ancient city of Corinth with a statement that is worthy of being a life verse: "Be steadfast, immovable, always abounding in the work of the Lord, knowing that in the Lord your labor is not in vain."

1 CORINTHIANS 15:58

02

The Voice That Whispers to You

The Holy Spirit is the third person of the Trinity as God's indwelling presence in our lives. The work of the Holy Spirit is to convict, comfort, teach, empower, and produce spiritual fruit in our lives. No wonder we are told to be filled with the Spirit of God.

The whisper of the Holy Spirit is that voice of conscience when you are open and willing to listen to God's leading. Conscience is the reminder of beliefs we know to be true. The Holy Spirit is our teacher but also our reminder of what we already know.

Need more encouragement to be filled with the Holy Spirit? "But the Helper, the Holy Spirit... will teach you all things and bring to your remembrance all that I have said to you."

JOHN 14:26

03

Truth on Trial

God is always the champion of justice, especially for those who are vulnerable and mistreated. God's heart goes out to the poor, the orphan, the widow, and the oppressed. These groups often lacked protection in ancient societies, and God demanded his people provide for them.

Justice isn't just about punishing wrong; it's about actively defending those without power. Societal laws provide our values for the framework for justice. How we live in awareness with a just response to these groups adds value in our community through Christlike actions. We act justly in the name of Jesus.

The lack of justice is not a new problem, but it is a continuing concern: "Give justice to the weak and the fatherless; maintain the right of the afflicted and the destitute."

PSALM 82:3

04

Strength Is Measured in Restraint

Self-control is discipline over desires, emotions, and actions. It's not about sheer willpower but about Spirit-empowered discipline. It is surrendering control to the Holy Spirit in that particular stronghold of your life. The more you yield to the Holy Spirit, the stronger your self-control becomes.

Self-control is included as a "fruit of the Spirit" to guard believers from sin and to help people live more wisely. Let the Spirit in you live out the quality of life you always dreamed of as you become more Christlike. This is all a reflection of the truth that you were created in the image of God. That image gets fuzzy at times because of life. Self-control helps bring clarity once again to a distorted image of God in your life and the work of the Holy Spirit through your life.

The pithy statements of the Proverbs always say it well: "A man without self-control is like a city broken into and left without walls."

PROVERBS 25:28

05

The Gospel Travels Person to Person

Evangelism is sharing the good news of Jesus Christ. It's not a program but an overflow of love. When people have a life-changing encounter with Jesus, they naturally want others to experience what it means to follow Jesus too.

Your story points to his story. Evangelism is about relationships. Build a credible relationship with a friend without any religious strings attached to the relationship. Just be friends and let who you are and how you live create an awareness that you are a follower of Jesus. Life will give you opportunities to earn the right to be heard by others when they bump into the brokenness of the world in their own life.

Saint Francis of Assisi is famous for saying: "Preach the Gospel at all times. If necessary, use words."

Here is the promise when your life positively touches another: "How beautiful are the feet of those who preach the good news!" Let your life preach more than your words...

ROMANS 10:15

06

Faith That Works
Is Faith at Work

Belief and action are two sides of the same coin. We are saved by grace alone. Once saved, we express our gratitude for God's mercy by serving the needs of others. In our New Covenant agreement with God, we demonstrate our love for God by how we relate to and love others.

At the end of Jesus' earthly ministry, he summarized the Ten Commandments. He had already given the executive summary in two key ideas: love God and love your neighbor. At the Last Supper during the Passover meal with his twelve disciples, Jesus gave a new commandment. He went from ten to two to one: "Love one another as I have loved you" (John 13:34).

How do we love others? When our faith leads to a variety of good works that touch the lives of other people. Salvation is by faith alone, but genuine faith produces an endless list of good works as evidence!

James connects faith and works in these words: "Some will say, you have faith; I have deeds. Show me your faith without deeds, and I will show you my faith by my deeds" (James 2:18).

JAMES 2:14-26

07

What Letters Did the Apostle Paul Write in the New Testament?
Part One

Paul is credited with writing nine letters to churches (and four to individuals). Paul sent letters to encourage churches to grow in maturity. He provided pastoral care to new believers, and he often addressed moral failures, conflicts, and false doctrines within churches. His letters applied the Gospel of Jesus to messy real-life situations.

Paul's letters to churches include:

Romans – Explains salvation by faith in Christ and its power to transform life.

1 Corinthians – Addresses problems in the church and calls believers to unity, holiness, and love.

2 Corinthians – Paul defends his ministry and teaches about God's strength in weakness.

Galatians – Declares freedom in Christ from the law, emphasizing salvation by grace through faith.

Ephesians – Celebrates the church's unity in Christ and calls believers to live out their new identity.

Philippians – A letter of joy, encouraging believers to live humbly and rejoice in Christ.

Colossians – Exalts Christ's supremacy as God and warns against false teaching.

1 Thessalonians – Encourages steadfast faith, hope, and love while awaiting Christ's return.

2 Thessalonians – Corrects misunderstandings about the Lord's return and urges perseverance.

PHILIPPIANS 1:3-8

08

What Letters Did the Apostle Paul Write in the New Testament?
Part Two

Paul is credited with writing four letters to individuals (and nine to churches). He wrote to Timothy on how to lead the church in Ephesus and to Titus on leading the church in Crete emphasizing sound doctrine, worship order, qualifications for leaders, and warnings against false teaching. When he wrote to Philemon, it was an appeal to forgive and welcome back his runaway slave, Onesimus, now a Christian brother. Paul's letters to individuals include:

1 Timothy – Guidance for church leadership, doctrine, and godly living.

2 Timothy – Paul's final letter, urging Timothy to remain faithful and courageous.

Titus – Instructions on appointing godly leaders and living out sound doctrine.

Philemon – A personal appeal for forgiveness and reconciliation through Christ.

2 TIMOTHY 2:2

09

What are the Other Letters in the New Testament?

Eight additional letters were written to a broader audience rather than to individual churches or people. They emphasize perseverance in trials, the call to live out genuine faith through good works, warnings against false teaching, and the centrality of love and truth in the Christian life. They provide a call to followers of Jesus to stand firm, love deeply, and remain faithful until Christ's return. These books include:

Hebrews – Exalts Jesus as the superior High Priest and perfect sacrifice, calling for steadfast faith.

James – Emphasizes living a faith expressed through good works.

1 Peter – Encourages suffering believers with hope in Christ and a call to holy living.

2 Peter – Warns against false teachers and reminds of Christ's promised return.

1 John – Assures believers of eternal life and calls them to walk in love and truth.

2 John – Urges truth, love, and rejection of false teaching.

3 John – Commends hospitality and faithfulness in supporting fellow believers.

Jude – Warns against ungodly influences and calls believers to contend for the faith.

COLOSSIANS 1:6

10

What Is John's Vision in Revelation?

The book of Revelation is attributed to the Apostle John near the end of his life, 90-95 A.D., when he was exiled on the island of Patmos. It was written to seven churches in Asia Minor (Turkey) representing both real congregations and symbolic of the universal church.

It was written to encourage persecuted Christians ensuring them that God is in control, evil will not prevail forever, and Christ will return to establish his Kingdom. It is both a warning to the unfaithful and a promise of hope to those who endure to the end.

Revelation is not just about the future. It also gives hope and perspective for the present day. Evil may appear to have the upper hand, but God is stronger. History is moving toward Christ's ultimate triumph in God's time and in God's way. Followers are called to stand firm in living with anticipation and confident hope of Christ's second coming.

"Blessed is the one who reads aloud the words of this prophecy and blessed are those who hear it and take to heart what is written in it, because the time is near."

REVELATION 1:3

11

Eternal Life Means Eternal Security

Salvation is secure because God is faithful and unchanging. We can change our mind, but God never does. Followers of Jesus can rest in God's promises and Christ's finished work on their behalf, not in their own efforts.

The assurance of salvation is not based on what we are feeling at any given moment nor is it based on how hard we work to make it to heaven. Our assurance is based on God's unchanging promise, Christ's finished work, and the Spirit's seal which marks followers of Jesus as God's own (2 Corinthians 1:21-22). This gives believers unshakable confidence that nothing can separate them from God's eternal love!

The Apostle John said it eloquently: "I write these things... that you may know that you have eternal life."

1 JOHN 5:13

12

Idleness Is Wasted Time Dressed Up as Rest

There is a rhythm given by God for a day of rest every seven days, but anything more is spiritual laziness or neglect of responsibilities as followers of Christ.

Idleness is more than inactivity. That's because it's more than doing nothing. It is the neglect of responsibility, wasting opportunity, or avoiding your God-given purpose and calling. The Bible contrasts idleness with diligence, wise living, and stewardship as managers of all the resources God has provided.

Idle hands open the door to temptation. When energy is not directed toward meaningful work, it can too easily be used in ways more negatively.

Paul gives this admonition to the church in the ancient city of Thessalonica: "If anyone is not willing to work, let him not eat."

2 THESSALONIANS 3:10

13

History Is His Story

Sovereignty is God's supreme rule and authority over all creation with wisdom, power, and purpose. Nothing happens outside his knowledge. He is not only the Creator but also the Sustainer and King. Even when the evil of the world seems to prevail, God is at work to accomplish his ultimate purpose in offering salvation from the power of sin to everyone including you.

God's sovereignty matters. It reminds us of our security even in times of uncertainty. Even when the world seems out of control, God weaves every event into his greater plan. Sovereignty reminds us that he is God and we are not. It is an appropriate expression in worship and praise referring to God as the Most High God.

The Psalm expresses it well: "Our God is in the heavens; he does all that he pleases."

PSALM 115:3

14

Think Differently, Live Differently

Renewing your mind is the result of replacing the world's thinking with God's wisdom. We do that in four ways:

Replacing lies with truth – Scripture is your lens to see life from God's perspective.

Changing patterns of thinking – Breaking habits of fear, worry, pride, or selfishness by training your mind toward gratitude, humility, and faith.

Redirecting desires – Moving from self-centered goals toward God's perfect will.

A daily reorientation of thinking – Renewal is not a moment but a lifelong journey of faith.

Paul tells us not to model our life by the values of this world, but to "Be transformed by the renewal of your mind, that by testing you may discern what is the will of God – what is good and acceptable and perfect."

ROMANS 12:2

15

Love Is the Tie That Binds

In the face of trials and failures, the promise of God's love is a reminder to us of who he is and who he created us to be. He is the God of second chances. His love never fails. He calls his people to live in light of his faithful presence in their lives. He never leaves us or forgets about us. This chapter in Paul's letter is a reminder of how powerful God's love at work in our lives can be: "Love bears all things, believes all things, hopes all things, endures all things."

1 CORINTHIANS 13:7

16

When it Costs You Something

Sacrifice is giving up something valuable for God's sake. Jesus gave the ultimate sacrifice. We are to follow Christ's example and live self-giving lives. It's an other-centered way of living. When we live for ourselves, sacrifice is not even a passing thought. We want others to sacrifice for us. When we choose to follow Jesus, we are called to a life of sacrifice. It means we give up what might be best for us in order to do what might be best for someone else. How could you sacrifice today for your family or for your co-workers?

Sacrifice is not an event. It's not a moment. It's all the time: "Present your bodies as a living sacrifice, holy and acceptable to God."

ROMANS 12:1

17

Pride Blinds When Humility Sees

Pride is an inflated sense of self over God and others. It's not just confidence; it is self-exaltation. At its worst, it is purposeful arrogance. It places self as number one in everything. Pride blinds people to correction, to truth, and to humility.

Narcissists live with an insatiable amount of pride. They are never wrong. They never apologize. In conflict there is only one way to understand what happened. They always win. You always lose. It is a psychological personality disorder. Can they change? Not without professional therapy and God's transforming power at work in them.

Over time pride keeps any of us from seeing our own faults. Pride creates permanent distance between people in conflict because reconciliation is always one-sided. It's only on their terms. Pride keeps life and relationships from what might have been.

The warning in Proverbs says: "Pride goes before destruction, and a haughty spirit before a fall."

PROVERBS 16:18

18

Back of the Line

Servant leaders lead by serving others. This approach challenges the traditional approach to leadership where senior leaders have the corner office, the reserved parking space, and the company's stadium suite to watch their favorite sports team.

In servant leadership, direct reports are not there to serve the leader and make him or her look good. The servant leader's primary responsibility is to develop each team member, so they are successful.

"Leaders eat last" is a military practice where officers let the soldiers eat first. Jesus modeled this kind of humility when he took a towel at the Passover Meal and did what a house servant always did for the guests: He washed their feet as it describes n John 13. Great leaders develop more leaders by modeling the attitude and the behavior of a servant.

Jesus was still teaching his team on the way to his trial and crucifixion in Jerusalem. They were arguing among themselves who would get positions of honor in Jesus' new Kingdom. They completely misunderstand the nature of the of God's other-centered kingdom where a top-down approach is completely reversed!

Jesus said: "Whoever would be great among you must be your servant."

MATTHEW 20:26

19

How to Build Bridges Not Walls

Reconciliation is the restoration of broken relationships. Christ's work on the cross reconciles us to God. Because of Jesus' example, we are also called to reconcile our relationships with others. It starts when someone is willing to forgive, even before the other person seeks reconciliation.

Hanging on to grudges destroys relationships even beyond the individual to a wider circle of mutual friends or their families. Reconciliation chooses love and forgiveness over getting even.

Both dimensions of reconciliation work hand in hand in God's Kingdom: "God... reconciled us to himself through Christ and gave us the ministry of reconciliation."

2 CORINTHIANS 5:18

20

I Want a Perfect Church

Unfortunately, the community of believers is made up of imperfect people. It's why the church can welcome anyone. We all come with flaws.

In the book of Hebrews, we are reminded why the church is important in our life of following Jesus. "And let us consider how we may spur one another on toward love and good deeds, not giving up on meeting together, as some are in the habit of doing, but encourage one another – and the more as you see the Day approaching" (Hebrews 10:24-25).

Why attend a community of faith every Sunday? The church is a gathering of God's people, empowered by the Spirit, who worship together, grow together, and serve together.

The Apostle Paul makes this declaration to every follower of Jesus: "Now you are the body of Christ and individually members of it."

1 CORINTHIANS 12:27

21

Worship Is the Emotional Side of Following Jesus

Worship is love expressed to God with surrendered hearts, a posture of humility, a purpose that resets "true north" in our life, and a community that thanks God together in one place at one time every week.

Worship is not just singing but a lifestyle of obedience, giving, and serving. It is a picture of uniting diverse people who join hands and hearts in the face of a divided world.

> *"I rejoiced with those who said to me,*
> *'Let us go to the house of the Lord.'"*

PSALM 122:1

22

Experience Teaches, Wisdom Applies

What: Knowledge is the information we gather.

So What: Understanding is grasping what that information means.

Now What: Wisdom is applying that knowledge and understanding in a way that deepens my faith and meets the needs of other people.

Wisdom begins with a sense of awe and humility before God: "The fear of the Lord is the beginning of wisdom."

PROVERBS 9·10

23

Stumbling Blocks

In the Bible, a stumbling block is anything that causes someone else to fall into sin, have doubt, or get caught in spiritual failure. Paul uses the term in Romans 14:13: "Make up your mind not to put any stumbling block or obstacle in the way of a brother or sister." This verse is an invitation to live in such a way that gives others a chance to grow in their relationship to Christ.

Matthew 18:6-7 is the flip side. It's a warning especially for children but it applies to any age. Do not cause others to sin. God will always hold us accountable. Jesus said: "But whoever causes one of these little ones who believe in me to sin, it would be better for him if a great millstone were hung around his neck and he were thrown into the sea. Woe to the world because of the things that cause people to stumble."

MATTHEW 18:6-7

24

The Great Commandment

Jesus summed up the whole Old Testament law in two of the ten commands. Love for God and neighbor are our highest calling.

Loving God by listening, learning, applying, being obedient, not using his name in vain, serving others in Jesus' name, living each day with nothing in life being more important than God, gratitude for his mercy and grace, trusting his timing and his ways, and connecting regularly in prayer.

Loving Neighbors through acts of kindness, hospitality, forgiveness, generosity, encouragement, advocacy, and the gift of time.

> *"You shall love the Lord your God...*
> *and your neighbor as yourself."*

MATTHEW 22:37-39

25

The Church on the Way

The Great Commission is God's call and mission for us to invite everyone to follow Jesus.

When your church is other-centered, then your immediate community is the starting place. Demonstrating God's love to the least of those in your hometown is how to love on your city. When you do it continually, it is noticed especially when you serve the needs that exist with no strings attached.

What ministries in your church are other-centered? Most likely those ministries don't happen on your campus. They happen where the needs occur day in and day out. Are you part of an other-centered serving team?

"Go therefore and make disciples..."

MATTHEW 28:19

26

The In-Between Time

We are living in the in-between time—between Christ's first coming and his second coming. Some call this time "already but not yet." God's Kingdom is already underway as announced by Jesus in his teaching and ministry. But the completion of the Kingdom in a new heaven and new earth has not yet been fulfilled.

Our invitation is not to build charts and timelines to estimate when Christ will return based on signs of the time indicated in the New Testament. Paul said it articulately in 1 Corinthians 1:7-8: "Therefore you do not lack any spiritual gift as you eagerly wait for our Lord Jesus Christ to be revealed. He will also keep you firm to the end, so that you will be blameless on the day of our Lord Jesus Christ."

What is your spiritual gift and how are you using it to support the work of your local church? How are you using your interests and talents to connect with people outside the church who live far from God?

Believers look forward with joy to the second coming but know we are to be faithful until that day comes. John touched on this too when he said: "...continue in him, so that when he appears we may be confident and unashamed before him at his coming."

1 JOHN 2:28

27

Greet One Another with a Holy Kiss

Yup! Kissing in church and not in the back row or balcony of the auditorium. Read about it: 1 Corinthians 16:20; 2 Corinthians 13:12; Thessalonians 5:26; 1 Peter 5:14.

In the first-century Mediterranean world, a kiss was a common cultural greeting like today's handshake, hug, or fist bump. Please note that Paul and Peter put a qualifier on the kissing. It's a holy kiss, certainly not suggesting a romantic kiss in church! A holy kiss, motivated by Christ's love, not by romantic passion or impropriety, symbolized unity, equality, and affection within the Christian community. It broke down divisions of class, status, and ethnicity. So start kissing next Sunday.

ROMANS 16:16

28

Spiritual Warfare

Spiritual warfare is the battle against sin, the flesh, and spiritual forces. Paul described it this way, "For our struggle is not against flesh and blood, but against the rulers, against the authorities, against the powers of this dark world and against the spiritual forces of evil in the heavenly realms" (Ephesians 6:12).

While we live in a physical world, our deepest battles are spiritual. We often try to resolve these spiritual issues with human self-help strategies like logic, will power, persuasion, or determination. These spiritual battles require spiritual weapons like prayer, Scripture, times of worship, and claiming the authority of Christ. These battles are won in God's power at work in us and through us.

"For though we live in the world, we do not wage war as the world does. The weapons we fight with are not the weapons of the world. On the contrary, they have divine power to demolish strongholds" (2 Corinthians 10:3-4).

In spiritual warfare, believers stand firm by putting on the armor of God. God gives us everything we need to stand up in the moments of temptation and to stand against the powers of evil and the strong-holds they create in our lives.

"Put on the whole armor of God..."

EPHESIANS 6:11

29

Your War Is Already Won

Jesus has already won the war against Satan who has already been defeated. The timeline of how Jesus has decisively broken Satan's authority includes the past, present, and future:

Past: Satan was defeated at the cross and the empty tomb. Colossians 2:14-15 says, Christ "disarmed the powers and authorities...triumphing over them by the cross." The cross paid the debt of sin, removed Satan's right to accuse us, and death lost it dominion and fear over us. Satan's defeat was final and irreversible.

Present: Satan is being defeated in the present moment. We fight a defeated enemy who can tempt, deceive, and influence, but he cannot own or separate believers from God. James 4:7 says, "Resist the devil and he will flee."

Future: Satan will be finally removed forever. His final defeat will be visible and complete in the end of this age. Romans 16:20 says, "The God of peace will soon crush Satan under your feet."

So fight from victory not for victory. "...he (Christ) made a public spectacle of them (powers and authorities), triumphing over them by the cross."

COLOSSIANS 2:15

30

We Are in this Together to the End

Fellowship within the Christian community is simply sharing life together in Christ. Fellowship fosters encouragement, support, accountability, and unity. It happens in corporate worship, small groups, and in shared serving opportunities within the community.

The church is not a building or an organizational structure. The word we translate as church literally means a gathering of people even if it's just two or three. God meets us in community according to Matthew 18:20. The regular experience of community with other Jesus' followers equips us for dealing with the best and the worst life throws at us.

In the early church in Jerusalem, the followers of Jesus met regularly: "They were devoting themselves to the apostles' teaching, to fellowship, to the breaking of bread, and to prayer." How devoted are you to a regular local gathering of likeminded followers of Jesus? It's not optional but a non-negotiable from Jesus' perspective.

ACTS 2:42

31

When Truth Defeats Temptation

Jesus went toe to toe with Satan in a historic battle of temptation in Matthew 4. Jesus' victory shows us three areas of temptation we will face: appetite, pride, and power. And Jesus used one strategy for his defense that we can use too. He corrected Satan each time he faced temptation by using God's Word. It is our source of truth. The ultimate outcome in the face of temptation is obedience to God.

Jesus pointed Satan to the words and wisdom from his Heavenly Father: "Man shall not live by bread alone, but by every word that comes from the mouth of God." Satan tried again, and Jesus said: "Do not put the Lord God to the test." Satan tried one last time, and Jesus said: "Worship the Lord your God, and serve him only." Then Satan left him, and he will leave us too.

MATTHEW 4:1-11

SEPTEMBER

THE CHURCH

"Christ is also the head of the church, which is his body. He is the beginning, supreme over all...so he is first in everything."

— COLOSSIANS 1:18

The Church

For the different ways we see you, for all the ways you move
All the colors and expressions, oh, the beauty of your church
What a masterful reflection when we are unified
Truly celebrate each other and let go of our pride
That you would have a spotless bride

We surrender our agendas, our preferences, our plans
Would you help us work together to be your feet and hands
Our heart is just to know you, to show them who you are
That the gospel's still the answer for every searching heart

We're brothers and we're sisters
It's under the banner of your Name
We're mothers and we're fathers
It's under the banner of your Name
And we're all your children
It's all for the glory of your Name

And we praise the Father and praise the Son
Oh Holy Spirit, come and make us one
From every nation, every tribe and tongue
This is our cry, your kingdom come

Every story of revival, every miracle we've seen
It's a glimpse of what is coming, o by faith help us believe
And we know the day is coming when we will see your face
Every knee will bow before you and every heart will say

Oh praise the Father, and praise the Son
Holy Spirit, come make us one
From every nation, every tribe and tongue
This is our cry, your kingdom come
Lord, hear our cry, let your will be done
This is our cry, your kingdom come[12]

01

Jesus Had a Bad Day

The temple in Jerusalem was the center of Jewish worship. At the Passover and other feasts, pilgrims came from all over the region to worship and offer sacrifices. To do this they needed animals for sacrifice and temple currency for offerings.

The merchants and money changers set up their business stands in the outer courts of the temple. This area was called the Court of the Gentiles. It was a space meant for prayer. This was one of the only times Jesus showed open, forceful, and righteous anger. He overturned the tables and said: "It is written, my house shall be called a house of prayer, but you are making it a den of robbers" (Matthew 21:13).

Jesus had a passion for the sanctity of worship and opposed anything that corrupted it. Do we? Jesus' actions were a call to restore pure worship, the priority of prayer, and access for all people to seek God.

**ISAIAH 56:7;
JEREMIAH 7:11**

02

It's Time to Remember
and Celebrate – Part One

The Spring Feasts in the Jewish year included several festivals commanded by God to commemorate specific acts of God in Israel's history:

Passover – A celebration of Israel's deliverance from Egypt.

Feast of Unleavened Bread – A week-long feast right after Passover symbolizing purity and the removal of sin.

Feast of First Fruits – A celebration of the first sheaf of the harvest, pointing to Christ as the "first fruits" of those who have fallen asleep (1 Corinthians 15:20).

Feast of Weeks – Also called Pentecost. It was fifty days after first fruits celebrating the wheat harvest and the giving of the law at Mount Sinai and it was fulfilled in Acts 2 with the release of the Holy Spirit to everyone who believed in Jesus as the Christ.

LEVITICUS 23:2

03

It's Time to Remember
and Celebrate – Part Two

The fall feasts in the Jewish year included more celebrations with the purpose of never forgetting what God had done. Every feast anticipates or reflects God's salvation through the coming Messiah.

Feast of Trumpets – Also called Rosh Hashanah, marked the blowing of shofar, calling people to repentance and looking forward to God's final gathering of his people.

Day of Atonement – Also called Yom Kippur, is the most solemn day with sacrifices for national atonement pointing to Christ as the ultimate and once for all sacrificial atonement.

Feast of Tabernacles – A week of rejoicing, remembering God's provision during Israel's wilderness wandering by living in booths. It pointed God "tabernacling" with his people.

NUMBERS 28-29

04

It's Time to Remember
and Celebrate – Part Three

Other Jewish festivals created a rhythm of corporate worship in Israel's life to keep God at the center of national and family life. These were visual teaching tools to teach future generations.

Purim – Celebrates God's deliverance in the book of Esther.

Hanukkah – Also called the Feast of Dedication or Lights. It remembers the rededication of the temple after its desecration by Antiochus IV in Daniel 8 and John 10:22.

Memorials - The Israelites often set up piles of stones not as objects of worship but markers of memory as visible testimonies that God had acted, promised, or delivered them. It is perhaps a practice we should do more of in our own adventures of following Jesus.

**JOSHUA 4:1-9; JOSHUA 8:30-32; 1 SAMUEL 7:12;
GENESIS 31:44-52; 2 SAMUEL 18:17-18**

05

The Armor of God

When Paul introduces this metaphor telling us to "put on the whole armor of God" in Ephesians 6:13, he is describing the spiritual resources that we need and that we can use for resisting evil.

Belt of Truth represents honesty, integrity, and grounding in God's truth.

Breastplate of Righteousness protects the heart symbolizing the ability to live rightly before God when we are covered by Christ's righteousness.

Shoes of the Gospel of Peace stand for readiness to share the good news. The shoes bring stability, direction, and peace during conflict.

Shield of Faith is used to extinguish fiery arrows of doubt, fear, and temptation.

Helmet of Salvation guards the mind and gives assurance of salvation.

Sword of the Spirit is the only offensive weapon on the list. It represents Scripture being used to resist lies and spiritual deception.

Paul ends this picture in Ephesians 6:18 with an invitation to "pray in the Spirit on all occasions with all kinds of prayers and requests."

EPHESIANS 6:10-18

06

The Sacred Value of Your Life and Every Life

We are all made in God's image. A commitment to the sanctity of life is the belief that all human life is valuable and worthy of protection because all life comes from God. This value has shaped Christian teaching on human dignity, ethics, and how we treat other people.

...We are created in God's image, Genesis 1:27

...God is the giver of life, Job 33:4; Psalm 139:13-16

...God prohibits murder, Exodus 20:13

The sanctity of life means every life matters to God and therefore must matter to us.

"For you formed my inward parts;
you knitted me together in my mother's womb."

PSALM 139:13

07

Marriage and Divorce

Marriage is designed as a lifelong covenant of love, faithfulness, and partnership under God. Divorce is permitted in the teaching in the Bible in some circumstances due to our human brokenness even though it is never the ideal. The call of the church and community is to uphold the beauty of marriage, while also extending grace, wisdom, and compassion to those navigating divorce.

> ...See organizations like Divorce Recovery Groups by Divorce Care: www.divorcecare.org

> ...See organizations like The Marriage Course by Alpha International: www.themarriagecourse.org

**GENESIS 2:24;
MALACHI 2:16**

08

Parenting Is a Marathon

Parenting is more than raising children into adulthood. It is shaping character, nurturing relational skills, and deepening spiritual roots to follow Jesus.

Parents are providers, protectors, teachers, coaches, and models. Parents are not designed to be their children's best friends because parenting means balancing love and discipline. Ultimately parenting is learning how to give roots and when to give wings to let go. The challenging transition is one of letting children become independent while finding ways to stay connected. For parent support resources see organizations like: www.connectedfamilies.org or, www.focusonthefamily.com.

Paul's challenge: "Bring them up in the discipline and instruction of the Lord."

EPHESIANS 6:4

09

Accountability with Other Followers

Accountability among followers of Jesus carries both encouragement and responsibility. Scripture teaches that we are part of one body in the church. We are called to carry one another's burdens in Galatians 6:2, and we are called to encourage one another daily in Hebrews 3:13.

The tougher part of accountability for one another is Jesus' call to confront sin with one another. Matthew 18:15-17 says to do this lovingly not to shame but to restore. James 5:16 takes it deeper in highlighting the importance of confessing sin to one another for spiritual healing.

A rule of the road is to earn the right to be heard. This needs to be done in genuine humility and confidentiality, not in self-righteous judgment. The motive is always restoration. If you don't have a genuine relationship then don't speak a word.

1 CORINTHIANS 13:1-2

10

A Sign of Spiritual Maturity

Spiritual growth is the journey of incremental steps in becoming more like Christ. The Apostle Paul describes spiritual growth in this insight: "So then, just as you received Christ Jesus as Lord, continue to live your lives in him, rooted and growing in him, strengthened in the faith as you were taught, and overflowing with thankfulness" (Colossians 2:6-7).

Those at the far end of the spiritual maturity continuum are able to look at the unanswered questions, the troubling inconsistencies, and the examples of hypocrisy in those whose walk doesn't always match their walk and still say, "Nevertheless, I trust in God."

ISAIAH 26:3-4

11

Gloria in excelsis Deo

These words are found in the angels' song that first Christmas. The words create the title in Latin to the traditional Christmas hymn known as *The Gloria* or *The Greater Doxology*. It is one of the oldest hymns of the Christian church.

...Gloria means glory

...In excelsis means in the highest

...Deo means to God

These are heavenly reminders of the God we worship and serve throughout the year not just in December: "Glory to God in the highest, and on earth peace, goodwill toward men."

LUKE 2:14

12

Life Verses #5 –
Hello God

*"This is the confidence that we have in approaching God:
that if we ask anything according to his will, he hears us.
And if we know that he hears us - whatever we ask -
we know that we have what we have asked of him."*

1 JOHN 5:14-15

13

God Has Your Tears in a Bottle

David, the writer of this Psalm, was reminded how much God cared for his situation even in his darkest hours. God kept David's tears in a bottle as a permanent reminder of him and his situation. In the same way God not only hears our prayers, but he knows and remembers our darker moments because he cares about us. He keeps your tears in a bottle as a reminder to surround you with his love during these times in your life. None of your tears are wasted or unnoticed by God.

"You keep track of all my sorrows.
You have collected all my tears in your bottle.
You have recorded each one in your book."

PSALM 56:8

14

God Cares Like the Best Mom Ever

The Bible uses maternal imagery to describe God's care resembling a mother who comforts, protects, and nurtures her child.

Isaiah said it this way, "Can a mother forget the baby at her breast and have no compassion on the child she has borne? Though she may forget, I will not forget you! Behold, I have engraved you on the palms of my hands..."

ISAIAH 49:15

15

Women in
Old Testament Leadership

Debora, Judges 4–5
A prophetess and judge of Israel. She led the nation both spiritually and militarily, guiding Barak to victory over Sisera. She is one of the clearest examples of great female leadership in Scripture.

Miriam, Exodus 15:20–21; Micah 6:4
The sister of Moses and Aaron. She was a prophetess who led Israel in worship after the Red Sea crossing.

Hulda, 2 Kings 22:14–20
A prophetess consulted by King Josiah's officials when the Book of the Law was rediscovered. Her authoritative message confirmed God's word for the nation.

Esther, Book of Esther
A queen who risked her life to intercede for her people and influenced the king's decision, leading to the salvation of the Jews from genocide.

Abigail, 1 Samuel 25
Though not a formal leader, her wisdom and courage prevented bloodshed by confronting David and appealing for peace. She influenced a future king.

ROMANS 12:8

16

Women in New Testament Leadership

Mary, Mother of Jesus, Luke 1–2; John 19
Chosen to bear the Messiah, her faith and obedience set an example of spiritual leadership. She was present with the disciples at Pentecost (Acts 1:14).

Mary Magdalene, John 20:11–18
The first witness of the resurrected Christ and sent by Jesus to tell the apostles—sometimes called the "apostle to the apostles."

Priscilla, Acts 18:24–26; Romans 16:3
Alongside her husband Aquila, she taught Apollos, a gifted preacher, more accurately about Christ. Paul calls them "fellow workers in Christ Jesus."

Phoebe, Romans 16:1–2
A deacon (servant/minister) of the church in Cenchreae. Paul entrusted her to deliver his letter to the Romans, showing her respected leadership role.

Junia, Romans 16:7
Mentioned as "outstanding among the apostles," showing recognition of her influence in the early church.

Lydia, Acts 16:14–15, 40
A wealthy businesswoman whose home became the first meeting place for the church in Philippi.

ROMANS 12:8

17

What's on the Inside Shows Outside

*"A happy heart makes the face cheerful,
but heartache crushes the spirit."*

PROVERBS 15:13

18

He Leads, We Follow

Psalm 23 begins describing God as the leader just like a shepherd with the sheep who follow:

He leads to **quiet waters**.

He leads to **green pastures**.

He restores our soul so he can also lead us in **paths of righteousness**.

He walks with us in the **dark valleys** of life.

He's honoring us in the sightline of our **enemies**.

His **goodness and love** follow us.

One day we will dwell in **his eternal home** forever.

PSALM 23

19

Joy Is the Echo of God's Presence

Joy is not circumstantial. That's happiness. Joy is cultivated in gratitude, sustained in trials, and strengthened in God's presence.

...Joy comes when we recognize God is near, regardless of life's ups and downs. Psalm 16:11, "In your presence there is fullness of joy."

...When joy is real, it naturally spills over into words, actions, and relationships. Romans 15:13, "May the God of hope fill you with all joy and peace as you trust in him."

...Joy isn't a denial of hardship. It's recognizing that trials produce endurance and maturity. James 1:2-3, "Consider it pure joy, my brothers and sisters, whenever you face trials of many kinds..."

Joy is not dependent on circumstances but flows from God's character and God's faithful and faith-filled promises.

> *"Though you have not seen him, you love him...*
> *you believe in him and rejoice with joy*
> *that is inexpressible and filled with glory."*

1 PETER 1:8

20

Unlikely Characters in God's Story
#1: Gideon

God often chooses and equips ordinary people for extraordinary purposes. Gideon's weakness became the stage for God's power.

He considered his clan of Manasseh the weakest among the twelve Hebrew tribes.

He saw himself as the least in his family within that tribe.

He asked for multiple signs from God before acting on God's call.

He hid in a winepress from his enemies, the Midianites, when God called him.

Even so, God called him to defeat the enemy, the Midianites. Interestingly, God kept reducing the number of troops from 32,000 to 300 who eventually would see victory not in human strength but in God's power.

You're not so ordinary after all. Just let God do his work in you and then through you to others.

JUDGES 6-8

21

Unlikely Characters in God's Story #2: Moses

God works through weakness, reluctance, and brokenness to accomplish his purposes.

...Moses was a foreigner in a different land than his family homeland.

...Moses was born in Egypt under Pharoah's rule. As a baby, he was hidden in a basket and floated on the river to avoid being killed. Baby Modes was found by the Pharoah's daughter and raised in that home.

...Moses was a fugitive after killing an Egyptian who was beating one of his own countrymen.

...Moses spent forty years in exile as a shepherd to shape his character as preparation for God's mission.

...Moses had a speech problem, "I am slow of speech and tongue" (Exodus 4:10).

...Moses led one of the greatest liberation movements in the Old Testament: The Exodus of an estimated two to three million Israelites from 400 years of slavery in Egypt.

God can use you for great things even if you have excuses why he wouldn't or shouldn't.

EXODUS 3-4

22

Living in the Shadow of the Cross

The cross was the Roman instrument of execution reserved for criminals, rebels, and slaves. Jesus was crucified in this most brutal of death sentences executed under Pontius Pilate's authority around 30-33 A.D.

Crucifixion was public and humiliating. Victims were stripped, nailed, or tied to the beams and left to die an agonizing slow death from exhaustion and eventually suffocation. The cross was both the darkest human act of violence and the greatest divine act of love.

The cross was God's plan for redemption of sin. Jesus satisfied the justice of God by taking the penalty we deserved for our own sin. The cross was the place where mercy and justice met. It is central to salvation, where sin was defeated and God's love was fully displayed. Jesus would have died for you had you been the only living person in the world. He loves you that much.

Paul message was always focused on one thing: "But we preach Christ crucified..."

1 CORINTHIANS 1:23

23

One God Worthy of Threefold Praise

The representation of the Trinity in the Bible describes one God in three persons — Father, Son, and Holy Spirit. It expresses God's unity and diversity: three distinct persons, yet one essence, working together in creation, redemption, and sanctification.

...The Father is not the Son.

...The Son is not the Spirit.

...The Spirit is not the Father.

None is greater or lesser, though they relate differently they are united in the work of salvation. It shows that God is relational by nature and love has always been the currency within the Trinity.

In Jesus' assignment for us to go into all the world, we represent one God in three persons: "Go therefore and make disciples of all nations, baptizing them in the name of the Father and of the Son and of the Holy Spirit."

MATTHEW 28:19

24

God Is More Powerful Than Any Superhero

God's power is unlimited and all-sufficient. His name, God Almighty, speaks of his supreme power, authority, and sovereignty.

Scripture emphasizes that God can do anything consistent with his character and his perfect will, from creating the universe to sustaining life and performing miracles.

> *"Ah, Lord God! It is you who have made the heavens and the earth by your great power... Nothing is too hard for you."*

JEREMIAH 32:17

25

God Knows Fully, Sees Clearly, and Guides Wisely

Johannes Kepler is credited with saying, "We are simply thinking God's thoughts after him."[13] His knowledge is complete, infinite, and perfect.

God knows the past, present, and future, including human thoughts and motives, which assures His perfect judgment and guidance. Nothing is hidden from him.

David said: "Even before a word is on my tongue, behold, O Lord, you know it altogether."

PSALM 139:4

26

Omnipresence of God

In Christian theology, one of God's attributes is his infinite presence. He is everywhere at all times. He is not bound by space or geography. He is fully present everywhere, all at once, without division or limitation.

There is no place where God is absent. His presence comforts believers because he is always near. It also reminds us that nothing is hidden from him. Try to hide from him. You can't. Try to hide anything from him? He knows. His presence may be a guardrail in your vulnerable moments, or a realization that you might as well come clean.

The book of Psalms expresses this truth: "Where shall I go from your Spirit? Or where shall I flee from your presence?"

PSALM 139:7

27

Heaven Came Down
2000 Years Ago

God becoming human in the person of Jesus Christ is called his "incarnation." It shows God's humility and love, as Jesus took on flesh to reveal God's very nature and provide salvation through his life, death, and resurrection.

God entered human history to see the brokenness of the world from our perspective and to let us see the reality of who God is as Creator and Redeemer from our perspective.

The mystery is that Jesus was fully God and fully human. By taking on human nature, Jesus lived a sinless life and died as a substitute on our behalf for the debt due for our sin, Philippians 2:6-8.

The Apostle John expresses it: "And the Word became flesh and dwelt among us, and we have seen his glory."

JOHN 1:14

28

Sometimes a Song Says it Best

You Say

I keep fighting voices in my mind that say I'm not enough
Every single lie that tells me I will never measure up
Am I more than just the sum of every high and every low?
Remind me once again just who I am because I need to know
Ooh-oh

You say I am loved when I can't feel a thing
You say I am strong when I think I am weak
And you say I am held when I am falling short
And when I don't belong, oh, you say I am Yours
And I believe, oh, I believe
What you say of me
I believe

The only thing that matters now is everything you think of me
In you, I find my worth, in you, I find my identity
You say I am loved when I can't feel a thing
You say I am strong when I think I am weak
And you say I am held when I am falling short
When I don't belong, oh, you say I am Yours
And I believe (I), oh, I believe (I)
What you say of me (I)
Oh, I believe

Taking all I have, and now I'm laying it at your feet
You have every failure, God, you have every victory[14]

1 JOHN 3:1

29

What Happened After Jesus' Resurrection?

Most dates are approximate. What happens in the first century is just the beginning of the Jesus' movement that has extended to every postal code everywhere.

A.D. 30-33. Resurrection, Holy Spirit comes at Pentecost.

A.D. 30-50s. Apostles spreading message of Jesus. Paul planted Gentile churches. Letters written to churches.

A.D. 50. Council of Jerusalem in Acts 15 resolves the question of the Gentile following Jesus without the requirements of Jewish law.

A.D. 60-90. Gospels and other New Testament documents are written.

A.D. 64. After the Great Fire of Rome, Emperor Nero persecuted Christians. Peter and Paul martyred.

A.D. 70. The destruction of Jerusalem and the Temple during the First Jewish-Roman War fulfilling Jesus' prophecy in Mark 13:1-2.

A.D. 90s. John writes the book of Revelation.

JOHN 21:25

30

The Day the Church Exploded

There were three centuries of persecution trying to crush this new Jesus' movement without success. Churches and copies of sacred documents were destroyed that would eventually become part of the Bible. For more than 250 years Christians faced imprisonment, torture, and execution for refusing to worship the emperor or the Roman idols.

Yet these earlier followers of Jesus stayed loyal to their faith. They forgave their persecutors and even sang and prayed at the executions of other followers of Jesus. These early followers of Jesus visited those in prison, helped the poor and took in abandoned babies who were unwanted. They nursed the sick during the plagues in spite of the threat of their own infection.

The compassion of these early Christians during this time of persecution and suffering won respect across the Mediterranean world as a contrast to the cruelty of the Romans who were doing the persecuting. That contrast damaged the credibility of Rome's anti-Christian policy. It wasn't until 313 A.D. when Constantine legalized Christianity in the Edict of Milan, that the church exploded. Scriptural documents could now be read, copied and distributed. In A.D. 393 the Council of Hippo and Carthage formally recognized the 27 books to be included in the New Testament. The Bible as we know it was completed by the end of the 4th century.

ACTS 28:28

OCTOBER

YOU ARE MY KING

"Now to the King eternal, immortal, invisible, the only God, be honor and glory for ever and ever. Amen."

— 1 TIMOTHY 1:17

You Are My King

I'm forgiven because you were forsaken
I'm accepted, you were condemned
I'm alive and well
Your spirit is within me
Because you died and rose again

Amazing love, how can it be?
That you, my king, would die for me
Amazing love, I know it's true
It's my joy to honor you
Amazing love how can it be?
That my king would die for me
Amazing love I know it's true
It's my joy to honor you
In all I do I honor you

That you, my king, would die for me
Amazing love, I know it's true
It's my joy to honor you
In all I do I honor you[15]

01

The Ten Biggest Questions Asked About Christianity #1: Does God Exist?

The BIG question: How can we know God is real? People wrestle with evidence for God's existence, proofs from creation, conscience, morality, and personal experience. A foundational answer is that creation, conscience, and reason point to God. Faith is not blind—it's a reasoned response to evidence of one's experience in a daily relationship with our Creator God.

The Apostle Paul states his case: "For since creation of the world God's invisible qualities – his eternal power and divine nature – have been clearly seen, being understood from what has been made, so that people are without excuse."

ROMANS 1:20

02

The Ten Biggest Questions Asked About Christianity #2: Can We Trust the Bible?

The BIG question: Can we trust the Bible as God's reliable Word? The question addresses historical accuracy in what the Bible reports, accurate transmission of documents through copying and translating, contradictions, and the significant question for all of us: Is the Bible still relevant today?

Archaeology, fulfilled prophecy, and manuscript evidence support its reliability. The Bible isn't just information—it's the revelation of God's wisdom for life transformation!

Peter adds this affirmation: "Above all, you must understand that no prophecy of Scripture came about by the prophet's own interpretation of things. For prophecy never had its origin in the human will, but prophets, though human, spoke from God as they were carried along by the Holy Spirit."

2 PETER 1:20-21

03

The Ten Biggest Questions Asked About Christianity #3: Who Is Jesus Really?

The BIG question: Was Jesus really God? Current debates focus on the deity of Christ, his claim to be God, miracles, and resurrection. Jesus' resurrection validates his claim to be God (John 11:25; John 20:28).

His resurrection was seen by hundreds of eyewitnesses whose lives were transformed. Their belief in Jesus as the Son of God led many to lose their lives as martyrs for this new Jesus' movement.

Christianity rises or falls on Jesus' identity and resurrection. The Apostle Paul made his case of the importance of Jesus' resurrection to the church in the city of Corinth: "And if Christ has not been raised, our preaching is useless and so is your faith...your faith is futile; you are still in your sins."

1 CORINTHIANS 15:14, 17

04

The Ten Biggest Questions Asked About Christianity #4: Why Is There Suffering and Evil?

The BIG question: If God is good and powerful, why is there so much suffering and injustice? This is one of the most common intellectual and emotional objections to following Jesus.

Evil exists because of human freedom. We are not puppets controlled by a grand puppet master in heaven. In our free will we have corrupted the perfect beginning that God offered in the Garden of Eden. God lets us experience the consequences of sin, and suffering is one outcome.

- Sometimes the consequences are fair because of our own choices of doing what God sees as sinful.
- Sometimes the consequences are not fair when they are caused by someone else's sinful choice.

No one has ever suffered the pain Jesus did in the brutality of a first-century crucifixion. He paid it forward for us for the forgiveness of sin. God allows us to pay forward the experience of suffering to the benefit of others. "Praise be to the God...who comforts us in our troubles, so that we can comfort those in any trouble with the comfort we ourselves receive from God."

2 CORINTHIANS 1:3-4

05

The Ten Biggest Questions Asked About Christianity #5: Is Jesus the Only Way to God?

The BIG Question: Is Jesus really the only way to God? What about other religions? People struggle with Christianity's claim of uniqueness and the idea of eternal separation from God.

Jesus said, "I am the way..." (John 14:6). He is the only God who died for our sins. Since Jesus is God, he is, in essence, saying that the only way to find me is the way I am providing freely in my death and resurrection on your behalf as a gift of salvation and forgiveness for you.

- Jesus is the only God who comes to you and serves you in his death and resurrection.

- Every other claim to deity asks you to be on an endless journey to find the divine.

- God doesn't make the life of the Spirit a mystery or a life-long journey without guarantees of ever arriving.

- God came in human form to make the Heavenly Father known to us in person.

- His invitation is simple: Come to me in order to find me. There is no other way.

Christianity is exclusive in its claim but inclusive in invitation. God loves the entire world. Your sin is never too sinful for God not to forgive. The biggest stumbling block is my need to admit that I am sinful, and I need a Savior to forgive my sin and close the gap between my imperfection and a holy God.

JOHN 14:6

06

The Ten Biggest Questions Asked About Christianity #6: Can Science and Christianity Coexist?

The BIG question: Doesn't science disprove Christianity? The topic includes: Evolution, creation, the age of the earth, miracles, and whether science and faith can coexist. Science explains how the world works; Christianity explains why it exists, (Psalm 19:1) and who created it all (John 1:3).

Faith and science are not enemies. They answer different questions. The Psalmist writes: "The heavens declare the glory of God; the skies proclaim the work of his hands. Day after day they pour forth speech; night after night they reveal knowledge."

PSALM 19:1-2

07

The Ten Biggest Questions Asked About Christianity #7: What Happens After We Die?

The Big question: Is there anything more after we die? There is continuing curiosity about eternity, judgment, heaven, hell, and whether everyone gets a second chance. In the Bible eternity is real, and our choices matter forever. We will all face judgment (Hebrews 9:27).

- If you follow Jesus and get to the end of your life and there is nothing more, what have you lost? Nothing except a moral life and a positive legacy.

- If you turn your back on God and live your own way as opposed to God's way, then there is another scenario. When you get to the end and find out that there is more beyond the grave that God has promised, then you've lost everything.

It's a wager. You bet one way or the other and live with the consequences. Jesus said it clearly. "I am the resurrection and the life. The one who believes in me will live, even though they die; and whoever lives by believing in me will never die."

JOHN 11:25-26

08

The Ten Biggest Questions Asked About Christianity #8: Why Are So Many Christians hypocrites?

The BIG question: Why do too many Christians say one thing but live differently? These questions arise from a number of situations:

- The unresolved conflict between Christians even in the same family.

- The moral failure among church leaders and members.

- The self-righteous attitudes by those who think they have arrived and are better than.

Christians are forgiven, not perfect (Romans 3:23). Becoming Christlike is a lifelong process of transformation. Followers of Jesus no longer live in sin but are still capable of giving into temptation in a broken and fallen world that surrounds them every day. Judge Christianity by Christ the only perfect human being who ever lived, not by His imperfect followers.

In the Sermon on the Mount, Jesus said: "You hypocrite, first take the plank out of your own eye, and then you will see clearly to remove the speck from your brother's eye."

MATTHEW 7:5

09

The Ten Biggest Questions Asked About Christianity #9: How Does Christianity Address Today's Moral Issues?

The BIG question: Does Christianity respond to modern issues like sexuality, justice, and freedom? People often wonder if Christian ethics are outdated or still authoritative, applicable, and possible today.

God's Word gives timeless wisdom for justice, sexuality, and relationships (Micah 6:8). Jesus final instructions to his followers summarize all Ten Commandments in one final command: "Love one another as I have loved you," John 13:34-35. In every relationship, in every conversation, in every situation, and in every decision, followers of Jesus ask: What does Jesus' kind of love require of me? Answering that leads to ethical living. Sometimes the answer between good and better or between bad and worse is the tension between what helps the most and hurts the least.

True freedom is living as God designed, not doing whatever we want. Ethics are timeless standards not relative suggestions for our situation at some point in time. The Old Testament prophet, Micah, said: "He has shown you, O mortal, what is good. And what does the Lord require of you? To act justly and to love mercy and to walk humbly with your God."

MICAH 6:8

10

The Ten Biggest Questions Asked About Christianity #10: What's the Purpose of Life?

The BIG question: What difference does Christianity make in my daily life? The questions include: understanding where I came from, why I am here, and where all of this is going to lead?

The heart of this question is the ultimate consideration: Does following Jesus give purpose, peace, perspective, and hope in a broken world? Solomon offered this statement of simple but profound wisdom in the close to his book of Ecclesiastes where he confronts the meaninglessness of life: "Here is the conclusion of the matter; fear God and keep his commandments, for this is the duty of all mankind. For God will bring every deed into judgment, including every hidden thing, whether it is good or evil" (Ecclesiastes 12:13-14).

Only in Christ do we find our ultimate meaning, peace, and lasting hope. Paul's writing in a letter to followers of Jesus in the city of Ephesus explains that we are not accidents; we are God's handiwork. Our lives were designed with intention as God has created meaningful works for us to live out. This is what he wrote to the Christ followers in the city of Ephesus: "For we are God's handiwork (masterpiece in some translations), created in Christ Jesus to do good works, which God prepared in advance for us to do."

EPHESIANS 2:10

11

Sometimes a Song Says it Best

"The Old Rugged Cross"

On a hill far away stood an old rugged cross, the emblem of suffering and shame; and I love that old cross where the dearest and best for a world of lost sinners was slain.

O that old rugged cross, so despised by the world, has a wondrous attraction for me; for the dear lamb of God left his glory above to bear it to, dark Calvary.

In that old rugged cross, stained with blood so divine, a wondrous beauty I see, for 'twas on that old cross Jesus suffered and died, to pardon and sanctify me.

To that old rugged cross I will ever be true, its shame and reproach gladly bear; then he'll call me some day to my home far away, where his glory forever I'll share.

So, I'll cherish the old rugged cross, till my troubles at last I lay down; I will cling to the old rugged cross, and exchange it some day for a crown.[16]

GALATIANS 6:14

12

Life's Trials Shape Heaven's Crown

The Crown of Life is an eternal reward for faithfulness to Christ. God promises this crown to those who endure trials and remain steadfast under pressure. Revelation 2:10 says, "Be faithful, even to the point of death, and I will give you life as your victor's crown."

The symbolic crown is a gift of grace but also a reward for perseverance in the Christian life. It doesn't mean salvation is earned by works. Salvation is by grace through faith. Enduring faith proves genuine love for God and receives heaven's honor.

James reinforces this truth and promise: "Blessed is the man who remains steadfast under trial... he will receive the crown of life."

JAMES 1:12

13

Law Sets the Standard.
Grace Supplies the Strength

There is a contrast and a connection between salvation by grace and works of the law. The law shows what a holy God requires. It is like a mirror that reflects our inability to perfectly measure up to God's holiness (Romans 3:20).

The law was never meant to save us from sin. It was meant to prepare the way for Christ (Galatians 3:24).

- The law without grace is a life of despair because it crushes us with guilt.

- Grace without the law is a distortion of God's reality.

- Without the law, grace could look like permission to keep sinning.

Together God's law and God's grace form the Gospel. The law drives us to see our need for Christ, and grace saves us and empowers us to live out what the law pointed to.

Grace provides forgiveness and righteousness through Christ alone. Galatians summarizes this truth: "We know that a person is not justified by works of the law but through faith in Jesus Christ."

GALATIANS 2:16

14

Life Verses #6 –
Wanting What You Already Have

When Paul was in prison, he was reflecting on the connection between his contentment and God's strength when he wrote a letter to the Christians in the city of Philippi.

- "I am not saying this because I am in need, for I have learned to be content whatever the circumstances. I know what it is to be in need, and I know what it is to have plenty. I have learned the secret of being content in any and every situation, whether living in plenty or in want" (Philippians 4:11-12).

- Paul adds this conclusion: "I can do all this through him who gives me strength" (Philippians 4:13).

Verse 13 is the foundation for the contentment expressed in verses 11 and 12. The key to the Christian life is not personal willpower but the empowerment of Jesus living in and through us.

- Contentment isn't circumstantial. It's learned through trust and experience with God.

- True peace never comes from wealth, comfort, or freedom, but from confidence in God's presence, pardon, provision, and protection.

- Christ gives us strength to remain steadfast, peaceful, and faithful regardless of conditions around us.

2 CORINTHIANS 12:9

15

God's Framework for Marriage – Part One

Who's first in marriage? Three options: he's first, she's first, or they are both first. Let's go back to the beginning:

...In Genesis 1:26–28, the man and woman are equally created in God's image.

...In Genesis 2:18–20, the woman is created to be an "Ezer" ("helper") for the man.

People easily assume that "helper" implies being "lesser than" or a subordinate to the other. The word is frequently used in the Old Testament to describe God as a "helper" to people. God is never inferior to the people he helps. Applied to marriage it describes a relationship of meaningful partnership, where both bring strength and indispensable support with equal value. (See comments on February 7, page 64, for more background).

In the New Testament, the Apostle Paul explains the marriage relationship in light of God's original design with an overarching principle: "Submit to one another out of reverence for Christ" (Ephesians 5:21). Marriage is all about mutual submission. So, Paul applies his overarching principle to each one:

..."Wives, submit yourselves to your own husbands as you do to the Lord..." (Ephesians 5:22–24). This was not news to the first century wife who lived in a male-dominated world.

..."Husbands, love your wives, just as Christ loved the church..." (Ephesians 5:25–33). This was shocking and revolutionary to the first century husband who only knew marriage relationships of dominance and submission.

EPHESIANS 5:21-33

16

God's Framework for Marriage – Part Two

What? Jesus' teaching about God's New Covenant was the beginning of God restoring creation to his original intentions. It affects the nature of our relationship with God and also every relationship in life as Paul explains in Galatians 3:28.

Paul's revolutionary message in that male dominated culture affirmed the equal value and dignity of women alongside men. Seeing each other through God's eyes makes it possible for couples to submit to one another out of reverence for Christ. That reflects God's original design for mutual partnership where reciprocal humility replaces dominance by one and submission by the other.

So What? We live this way out of reverence for Christ, not merely respect for one another. Jesus modeled an other-centered way of living in a self-centered world. Christian marriage works when both people submit first to Jesus and, as a result, they learn to submit to one another.

Couples who celebrate their common ground as well as embracing their differences are living out what God originally intended. Roles and responsibilities are agreed to by one's gifting, maturity, strengths, availability, wisdom, and interest, rather than by rigid gender stereotypes and expectations. Then husbands and wives take turns on any remaining responsibilities neither naturally prefers or does well.

Now What? Paul ends his discussion with a summary of this overarching principle of mutual submission: "However, each one of you also must love his wife as he loves himself, and the wife must respect her husband" (Ephesians 5:33).

Mutual submission means that marriage is a "New Covenant" relationship where I am willing to say "no" to myself in order to say "yes" to my spouse.

Post Scriptum (P.S.) Submission never means remaining in an abusive or dangerous situation under the assumption that you are supposed to submit.

GALATIANS 3:28; GENESIS 1–3

17

Conflict Is Inevitable.
Combat Is Optional.

Some well-known personalities in the Bible found themselves in interpersonal conflict.

Cain and Abel – Genesis 4

Jacob and Esau – Genesis 25-33

Joseph and Brothers – Genesis 37-50

Moses and Pharoah – Exodus 5-14

David and Goliath – 1 Samuel 17

Paul and Barnabus – Acts 15:36-41

Euodia and Syntyche – Philippians 4:2-3

Philemon and Onesimus – Philemon 8-21

You cannot control the other person, but you can control yourself. Forgiveness breaks the cycle of being on the defense or the offense against someone else. A guardrail to prevent unresolved fights: "A gentle answer turns away wrath, but a harsh word stirs up anger."

PROVERBS 15:1

18

Benedictions Are Blessings.
Old Testament #1

Benedictions are short words of encouragement usually spoken at the close of worship, special events, and at the end of letters written to individuals or churches. They represent divine blessings spoken over believers. In the Old Testament, they emphasize faithfulness to God's Covenant relationship with the Hebrew, Israel nation. They are intended to pronounce God's favor, peace, and presence over his people.

The Aaronic Blessing is the priestly blessing, asking God to guard His people, show them favor, and grant them his peace. It assures Israel that God's presence is both protective and gracious: "The Lord bless you and keep you; the Lord make his face shine on you and be gracious to you; the Lord turn his face toward you and give you peace."

NUMBERS 6:24-26

19

Benedictions Are Blessings.
Old Testament #2

Benedictions are short words of encouragement usually spoken at the close of worship, special events, and at the end of letters written to individuals or churches. They represent divine blessings spoken over believers. In the Old Testament, they emphasize faithfulness to God's Covenant relationship with the Hebrew, Israel nation. They are intended to pronounce God's favor, peace, and presence over his people.

The Blessing of Moses reminds Israel of their unique identity as God's redeemed people, emphasizing joy, security, and God's victory on their behalf: "Happy are you, O Israel! Who is like you, a people saved by the Lord, the shield of your help and the sword of your triumph!"

DEUTERONOMY 33:29

20

Benedictions Are Blessings.
Old Testament #3

Benedictions are short words of encouragement usually spoken at the close of worship, special events, and at the end of letters written to individuals or churches. They represent divine blessings spoken over believers. In the Old Testament, they emphasize faithfulness to God's Covenant relationship with the Hebrew, Israel nation. They are intended to pronounce God's favor, peace, and presence over his people.

Many Psalms close with benediction-like statements. This closing line in the psalm acknowledges God's eternal reign and invites worshippers to join in praise that never ends: "Blessed be the Lord, the God of Israel, from everlasting to everlasting! Amen and Amen."

PSALM 41:13

21

Benedictions Are Blessings.
New Testament #1

Benedictions are short words of encouragement usually spoken at the close of worship, special events, and at the end of letters written to individuals or churches. They represent divine blessings spoken over believers. In the New Testament, they focus on grace, peace, sanctification, and the presence of Christ and the Spirit. They are often used at the end of worship services today as a way to send Jesus' followers out with the assurance of God's faithful presence in their lives.

Paul's Classic Benediction closes his letter with a reminder that all Christian living depends on the unearned grace and kindness of Jesus: "The grace of the Lord Jesus Christ be with you."

1 CORINTHIANS 16:23

22

Benedictions Are Blessings.
New Testament #2

Benedictions are short words of encouragement usually spoken at the close of worship, special events, and at the end of letters written to individuals or churches. They represent divine blessings spoken over believers. In the New Testament, they focus on grace, peace, sanctification, and the presence of Christ and the Spirit. They are often used at the end of worship services today as a way to send Jesus' followers out with the assurance of God's faithful presence in their lives.

In another of Paul's Benedictions he prays that God himself would transform believers fully and reassures them that God's faithfulness guarantees their growth and protection: "Now may the God of peace himself sanctify you completely... he who calls you is faithful; he will surely do it."

1 THESSALONIANS 5:23–24

23

Benedictions Are Blessings.
New Testament #3

Benedictions are short words of encouragement, usually spoken at the close of worship, special events, and at the end of letters written to individuals or churches. They represent divine blessings spoken over believers. In the New Testament, they focus on grace, peace, sanctification, and the presence of Christ and the Spirit. They are often used at the end of worship services today as a way to send Jesus' followers out with the assurance of God's faithful presence in their lives.

This rich blessing of the Apostle Paul invokes all three persons of the Trinity, affirming the grace, love, and fellowship that unite God's people: "The grace of the Lord Jesus Christ and the love of God and the fellowship of the Holy Spirit be with you all."

2 CORINTHIANS 13:14

24

Benedictions Are Blessings.
New Testament #4

Benedictions are short words of encouragement usually spoken at the close of worship, special events, and at the end of letters written to individuals or churches. They represent divine blessings spoken over believers. In the New Testament, they focus on grace, peace, sanctification, and the presence of Christ and the Spirit. They are often used at the end of worship services today as a way to send Jesus' followers out with the assurance of God's faithful presence in their lives.

Hebrews Benediction:
The writer prays for believers to be empowered by the resurrecting God to live in obedience and carry out his purposes. "Now may the God of peace who brought again from the dead our Lord Jesus... equip you with everything good that you may do his will."

HEBREWS 13:20-21

25

Benedictions Are Blessings.
New Testament #5

Benedictions are short words of encouragement usually spoken at the close of worship, special events, and at the end of letters written to individuals or churches. They represent divine blessings spoken over believers. In the New Testament, they focus on grace, peace, sanctification, and the presence of Christ and the Spirit. They are often used at the end of worship services today as a way to send Jesus' followers out with the assurance of God's faithful presence in their lives.

In Jude's Benediction he emphasizes God's sustaining power, preserving believers and ultimately presenting them in joy and perfection before his throne in heaven: "Now to him who is able to keep you from stumbling and to present you blameless before the presence of his glory with great joy... be glory, majesty, dominion, and authority, before all time and now and forever. Amen."

JUDE 24-25

26

Benedictions Are Blessings.
New Testament #6

Benedictions are short words of encouragement usually spoken at the close of worship, special events, and at the end of letters written to individuals or churches. They represent divine blessings spoken over believers. In the New Testament, they focus on grace, peace, sanctification, and the presence of Christ and the Spirit. They are often used at the end of worship services today as a way to send Jesus' followers out with the assurance of God's faithful presence in their lives.

Revelation's Closing Benediction is the last verse of Scripture. It assures believers that God's grace is the final word, sustaining his people until the end of time: "The grace of the Lord Jesus be with all. Amen."

REVELATION 22:21

27

Unlikely Characters in God's Story #3: Rahab

Her past did not define her. She was just surviving in the red-light district of Jericho. She hid the Hebrew spies, and it changed everything. There is something in her story for all of us.

1. She believed in something or someone beyond her current circumstances. Her faith saw beyond the present, Joshua 2:9-11.

2. She had the courage to risk everything even with just a simple faith in God, Joshua 2:4-6.

3. God's redemption and forgiveness took her from shame to significance. God is always able to rewrite your story, Matthew 1:5; Hebrews 11:31.

"Joshua spared Rahab...with her family...
because she hid the men Joshua had sent as spies to Jericho."

HEBREWS 11:31

28

Unlikely Characters in God's Story #4: The Samaritan Woman

When you get to give Jesus a drink of water everything changes. She is the woman at the well in John 4:1-42. Jesus meets her there in his travels through the unfriendly land of Samaria. Jesus demonstrated respect to her as a woman and as a Samaritan. That was not typical.

Jesus knew all about her questionable life. She isn't condemned just invited to consider a God whose worship is not tied to special sacred places where she would not be welcome anyway.

Worshipping God is more about spirit and truth. Jesus treated her with love and gave her hope in spite of her gender, ethnicity, and issues of personal morality. She realized that Jesus was the Messiah the Jews had long awaited. She became the first recorded evangelist bringing many to meet Jesus.

"Come, see a man who told me everything I ever did. Could this be the Messiah?"

JOHN 4:29

29

Unlikely Characters in God's Story #5: The Thief on the Cross

When Jesus was crucified, he was placed between two thieves in Luke 23:32-33. One of the thieves joined others in mocking Jesus. The other thief admitted his guilt and recognized Jesus' innocence. He turned to Jesus and said, "Jesus, remember me when you come into your kingdom" (Luke 23:42). Jesus said, "Truly I tell you, today you will be with me in paradise" (Luke 23:43).

There is always hope. It's never too late to believe. Even at the end of our lives God will forgive.

ROMANS 10:9-10

30

Life Verses #7 –
A Powerful Invitation

*"Love the Lord your God with all your heart
and with all your soul and with all your strength."*

DEUTERONOMY 6:5

31

Trick or Treat?

If you are following this daily reading in line with the calendar, then it is the night before All Saints Day. In its history, All Hallows' Eve became Halloween. Trick-or-Treating, costumes, Jack-o'-Lanterns, decorations, and parties are some of the modern traditions. In its early roots, this day marked the end of the harvest season and the beginning of winter. It was a time when people believed the boundary between the living and the dead was blurred.

For Christians, Halloween can serve as a reminder of the victory of light over darkness. All Saints' Day celebrates those who followed Christ faithfully in their lives, and All Souls' Day honors those who have departed from this life.

The New Testament is well aware of the war we face against "the powers of this dark world and against the spiritual forces of evil in the heavenly realms" (Ephesians 6:12). The Apostle Paul had seen it all in his Mediterranean travels to start new churches. He wrote, "Do not quench the Spirit...but test them all; hold on to what is good, reject every kind of evil" (1 Thessalonians 5:17).

John added this: "Dear friends, do not believe every spirit, but test the spirits to see whether they are from God"

1 JOHN 4:1

NOVEMBER

LIVING HOPE

"Praise be to the God and Father of our Lord Jesus Christ! In his great mercy he has given us new birth into a living hope through the resurrection of Jesus Christ from the dead."

— 1 PETER 1:3

Living Hope

How great the chasm that lay between us
How high the mountain I could not climb
In desperation I turned to Heaven
And spoke your name into the night
Then through the darkness, your loving kindness
Tore through the shadows of my soul
The work is finished, the end is written
Jesus Christ, my living hope

Who could imagine so great a mercy
What heart could fathom such boundless grace
The God of ages stepped down from glory
To wear my sin and bear my shame
The cross has spoken I am forgiven
The King of Kings calls me His own
Beautiful Savior, I'm Yours forever
Jesus Christ, my living hope

Then came the morning that sealed the promise
Your buried body began to breathe

Out of the silence the roaring lion
Declared the grave has no claim on me
Jesus Yours is the victory

Hallelujah, praise the One who set me free
Hallelujah, death has lost its grip on me
You have broken every chain
There's salvation in your name
Jesus Christ, my living hope[17]

01

Understanding God

Theology is the study of God. To understand who God is, start by answering these questions:

1. Who is God really in his essential character?

2. What is God's heart toward me?

3. What does God want my life to look like?

4. Can God be trusted?

5. How does God speak today?

6. Why did God create us?

7. Who is Jesus as God?

8. What is God doing about evil and injustice?

9. What does God promise about the future?

10. How do I love God with all my heart, soul, mind, and strength?

"Who is a God like you, who pardons sin and forgives the transgression of the remnant of his inheritance? You do not stay angry forever but delight to show mercy.

MICAH 7:18

02

Jesus' Last Words

1. The church is to "Go make disciples." The Great Commandment tells us how to do that: "Love your neighbor" (Matthew 22:37-40). The church is not only the church when we meet together in the same place at the same time. We are also the church in our community when we leave the church building and live out God's love and amazing grace at home, in school, around work, and anywhere in the community. We all have our own networks of relationships which is where we influence others to consider following Jesus.

2. The church is to meet regularly to "teach them (people who choose to follow Jesus) to obey all I have commanded you" (Matthew 28:19-20). Tim Keller's *New City Catechism* is built around 52 questions that address the basics beliefs of the Christian faith.[18] The questions are organized in three sections:

   a. God, Creation, and Fall,

   b. Christ, Redemption, and Grace,

   c. Spirit, Restoration, and Growth.

Does your church have a teaching plan to provide an overview of basic beliefs for children, youth, and adults? The first church in Jerusalem got it right: "They devoted themselves to the apostles' teaching and to fellowship, to the breaking of bread and to prayer."

ACTS 2:42-47

03

Toxic People

Family, friends, and co-workers can be toxic for a variety of reasons including those who act or react out of their woundedness. Tough love creates boundaries and separations in these relationships. Rather than enabling their toxic behavior we create space that is not only good for us but eventually for them too. If we tolerate that behavior, they rarely change on their own. If we create space, it provides an opportunity to confront their behavior and their need for change.

The people you spend time with can either build you up or pull you down. Influence is contagious as character leaks both positively and negatively. We become like those we repeatedly associate with. Guard your relationships. Not everyone should have access to your heart. This is not easy at work, but you can minimize the negotiable times during your workday to keep your distance. Paul offers this warning related to false teaching in the church: "Do not be misled: Bad company corrupts good character."

1 CORINTHIANS 15:33

04

Why Did Jesus Need to Pray?

The longest prayer in the Gospels is Jesus' prayer just before he was arrested and then went to an unfair trial before being crucified.

> ...Jesus prays for himself, John 17:1-5. He prays for a personal willingness to complete the work his Heavenly Father asked him to do.

> ...Jesus prays for His disciples, John 17:6-19. He prays for their unity and protection.

> ...Jesus prays for all believers, John 17:20-26. He prays for our unity across borders and cultures.

The themes in Jesus' prayer in John 17 include: glory, unity, protection, sanctification, and love. Jesus reveals what is most important in his heart: His relationship with the Father, his care for his disciples, and his desire for all believers to be united in love and truth. If the church is not united how can we expect our society to be united?

Jesus prayed: "That they may all be one; just as you, Father, are in me, and I in you, that they also may be in us, so that the world may believe that you have sent me."

JOHN 17:21

05

Sometimes a Song Says it Best

I Was Made for More

I know who I am 'cause I know who you are
The cross of salvation was only the start
Now I am chosen, free and forgiven
I have a future and it's worth the living

'Cause I wasn't made to be tending a grave
I was called by name
Born and raised back to life again
I was made for more
So why would I make a bed in my shame
When a fountain of grace is running my way?
I know I am yours, and I,
was made for more.

Hallelujah, you called out my name
So, I'll sing out your praise
Hallelujah, you buried my past,
I'm not going back
I know I'm yours, and I was made for more.[19]

REVELATION 19:1

06

Shepherding

"I am the good shepherd. The good shepherd sacrifices his life for the sheep" (John 10:11). This is one of the most comforting and relational images Jesus used of himself.

...He sacrifices himself for the sheep (John10:11, 15, 17-18).

...He knows his sheep personally (John 10:3).

...His sheep know his voice and follow him (John 10:4, 14, 27).

...He protects and provides for his sheep (John 10:9-10).

...He unites his flock (John 10:16).

Jesus owned this assignment of shepherding as central in his calling and ministry: "I am the good shepherd. The good shepherd lays down his life for the sheep."

JOHN 10:11-18

07

When Is Religious Teaching off Track?

The Bible repeatedly warns believers to discern and reject teachings that contradict Scripture. Even in the First Century, there were those who distorted God's truth for personal gain or deception.

The challenge today is to keep the main thing, the main thing: The cross of Christ and the resurrection of Jesus. In all our varying faith traditions we incorporate our own version of important areas of theology that surround the main thing. These are always interesting discussions among those who love to get into the theological weeds.

Sometimes our disagreements and effort put into convincing others who do not interpret the key biblical passages of these theological sidebars as we do, creates confusion and frustration to most of those who attend church or especially those who don't attend for that reason. The early church needed to be reminded to keep the main thing the main thing: "We should not make it difficult for the Gentiles who are turning to God" (Acts 15:19).

False teachers are always trying to distort the main thing. When they show up, the cross and the resurrection are the benchmark of true faith. Peter adds to the warning, "There will be false teachers among you, who will secretly bring in destructive heresies."

2 PETER 2:1

08

When Is Religious Teaching on Track?

Sound doctrine protects the church from error and builds believers up in truth and holiness. Pastors and churches are called to teach faithfully to the truth of Christ crucified and the resurrection for the salvation of the whole world that God loves.

...Communicate what was said with clarity and conciseness.

...Communicate what it means in light of the meaning in its original context to its original audience.

...Communicate the application principles that transcend times, places, and people.

Timothy saw the potential problem: "The time is coming when people will not endure sound teaching... but having itching ears they will accumulate teachers to suit their own passions."

2 TIMOTHY 4:3

09

When God Moved in Next Door

"The Word became human and made his home among us. He was full of unfailing love and faithfulness. And we have seen his glory, the glory of the Father's one and only son" (John 1:14). The idea that God stepped into our story in the flow of human history and lived among us is one of the most powerful teachings in Christian faith.

This makes Christianity unique among all world religious beliefs. God comes to us. In other religions the deity demands that we find them and come to them. Many religions teach that the human journey is a lifelong effort to reach, discover, and find favor with the divine. Their emphasis is often on people seeking God rather than the Christian God who seeks people.

JOHN 1:1-18

10

It's an Upside-Down Kingdom

Jesus' teaching was counter-cultural from centuries of traditions of how the world works.

...Love your enemies, Matthew 5:44 and Luke 6:27-28

...The first will be last, Mark 9:35 and Matthew 20:26-27

...Blessed are the poor in spirit, Matthew 5:3-12 and Luke 6:20-23

...Forgive 70 x 7, Matthew 18:21-22 and Luke 17:3-4

...Turn the other cheek, Matthew 5:39 and Luke 6:29

...Lose your life to save it, Mark 8:35 and Luke 9:24

...The greatest must become like a child, Matthew 18:3-4 and Mark 10:14-15

...Invite those who cannot pay you back, Luke 14:12-14

...Give to receive, Luke 6:38 and Acts 20:35

...Humility over arrogance, Luke 14:11 and Matthew 23:11-12

...Faith of a mustard seed, Mark 4:30-32 and Luke 13:18-19

MATTHEW 5-7

11

Discipline in the Church

There are times when loving accountability is needed within the community of faith. The reasons include: Restoring those in sin, protecting the congregation, and honoring God's standard of holiness. These conversations should always begin with an attitude of humility and confidentiality.

...First, the process always starts in private to protect the dignity and reputation of all involved.

...Second, bring a third party into the conversation as an objective witness of what is being said and done.

...Third, tell the church to understand exactly what is being done to prevent gossip and rumor.

...Finally, if necessary, separate them from the church (Matthew 18:15-17).

The motivation is restoration of the individual with the church or with other church members (Galatians 6:1). The reason is to protect the church's unity and reputation within the community in order to protect the church from division, false teaching, destructive behavior, and public scandal that damages everyone's reputation.

"If your brother sins against you, go and tell him his fault...
If he listens to you, you have gained your brother."

MATTHEW 18:15

12

Caring for Widows or Widowers

The value of Christian community is the care for those in times of their need. When an individual loses their spouse and they are left to themselves, life becomes lonely. The church can become their family. The Bible calls God's people to defend and care for widows as one example representing the vulnerable in society.

Living alone while getting older leads to vulnerability. It is true today of aging men and women who live alone. Men tend to withdraw to themselves more than women. That's when they get lonelier and as a result more vulnerable in trusting others when perhaps they should not.

> How does your church do congregational care for the aging and those alone?

> ...In family-oriented congregations, is there a place for singles of all ages?

> ...If you live alone, have you withdrawn more than is healthy for you?

The brother of Jesus saw him take time for interruptions in reaching out to the least of these in society. In leading the first church in Jerusalem, he had learned the Jesus' lesson of caring for those who can easily be overlooked "Religion that is pure and undefiled before God...is this: to visit orphans and widows in their affliction."

JAMES 1:27

13

Caring for Orphans

Protecting and nurturing children without parents. God is described as a Father to the fatherless, and he commands his people to mirror his compassion by protecting and nurturing children without parents.

Organizations like *Faith Bridge Foster Care* or *Bethany Christian Services*, one of the largest Christian adoption and family service agencies in the world, offer faith-based foster care and adoption resources. *Lifeline Children's Services and Project 1.27* in Colorado offer foster care training and support to churches and families.

God values this from his perspective in heaven, and we can take action here on earth: "A Father to the fatherless, a defender of widows, is God in his holy dwelling."

PSALM 68:5

14

A Season for Gratitude

The fourth Thursday of November is the American holiday called Thanksgiving. Later in this month people gather with family and friends when everyone around the table shares something they are thankful for.

Consider Ann Voskamp's practice that she does the other 364 days of the year. Her book records her journey of gratitude: *One Thousand Gifts: A Dare to Live Fully Right Where You Are*.[20] She invites the reader to embrace everyday blessings and begin an adventure of thankfulness by chronicling God's gifts. She came up with 1000 blessings and is still adding to her daily list.

> *"Give thanks to the Lord, for he is good,*
> *his love endures forever."*

PSALM 107:1

15

The Poor Will Always Be Among You

God calls his people to share with the poor, showing mercy and reflecting his heart for justice. It means giving freely to those in need while being mindful of those who live irresponsibly at the expense of others. The Bible distinguishes between tithes and offerings.

Tithe. It is giving the first 10% of one's income to God through their local church. It is seen as an act of obedience, stewardship, and the acknowledgment that all we have belongs to God.

Offering. It is anything given to God beyond the tithe. Offerings are voluntary gifts given from one's heart as an expression of gratitude, worship, and generosity.

Churches initiate ministries that meet the needs of the poor. These funds are "tithe" funds designated in the annual budget of the local congregation that members donate to make possible. Individuals can also give to these needs through local organizations that are targeted to this community need. These are "offering" funds given over and above their tithe to their church.

Organizations like *Love INC*, Love in the Name of Christ, collaborate with local churches in a community to validate needs and coordinate the services. When churches work together rather in silos to meet the community needs of hurting people, there is greater effectiveness and efficiency.

> *"Whoever is generous to the poor lends to the Lord,*
> *and he will repay him for his deed."*

PROVERBS 19:17

16

Justice at Work

God condemns dishonest practices and delights in integrity in all economic dealings when fairness and honesty are one's branding and reputation in the marketplace. Where might injustice take place in your community? Can you be a voice in calling it out? In your own business transactions personally or as a business, don't.

"A false balance is an abomination to the Lord,
but a just weight is his delight."

PROVERBS 11:1

17

How Are You Talking?

Believers are called to avoid lies and deceit, speaking truth with honesty and integrity as a reflection of God's nature. Lying can make awkward situations easier for now but much more difficult as time goes on while continuing the cover up.

Followers of Jesus always do the right thing regardless of the consequences. If you pay the price of honesty now, it is less expensive than having to pay it later. One wise woman once said, "Be sure your sins will find you out." Whether that happens or not, God knows.

"Having put away falsehood,
let each one of you speak the truth with his neighbor."

EPHESIANS 4:25

18

Avoiding Gossip and Rumor

Refuse to spread harmful or idle talk. It's easy to do with a long list of reasons, but it is a destructive waste of time.

- Gossip is spreading things true about another that you should keep to yourself.

- Rumor spreads information that is not true about another to damage their reputation to your own benefit.

Both gossip and rumor damage relationships in families and in business. God calls His people to use words that build up one another rather than the easier tendency to tear others down to make oneself look better.

It is clear in the proverb: "A dishonest man spreads strife, and a whisperer separates close friends."

PROVERBS 16:28

19

Self-Control Every Time You Open Your Mouth

The tongue has the power to bless or curse, so believers must use it wisely under the Holy Spirit's guidance.

Emotional intelligence is the ability to let the thinking side of the brain filter the emotional side of the brain. In moments of justified anger or frustration, pause to ask yourself if this is the time, place, person, and level of intensity with which to express what you are feeling just now?

> ...Be aware of what you are feeling. Emotions are normal signals of our response to what just happened.

> ...Be mature in your self-control to manage your words. The pregnant-pause can allow you time to choose how to respond rather than to react in the emotions of the moment.

> ...You'll never get in trouble for something you never said.

"The tongue is a small member,
yet it boasts of great things... it is a fire."

JAMES 3:5-6

20

Acts of Kindness

Kind acts are demonstrations of goodness and compassion to others. Kindness is both commanded and it is a fruit that the Holy Spirit produces in us. Kindness reflects God's character in daily interactions. Some refer to them as Random Acts of Kindness. Followers of Jesus would say, "Kindness is not random. It is the intentional way we live every moment of every day to represent the love of Christ."

If you had the opportunity to demonstrate God's compassion to someone today, who would it be and what could you do? The consistency of small acts of kindness is evidence of being a person of active compassion. Paul describes our motivation to live this way in one part of his letter to the Christians in the city of Ephesus: "Be kind to one another, tenderhearted, forgiving one another, as God in Christ forgave you."

EPHESIANS 4:32

21

Gentleness

Gentleness is strength under control in toxic moments. When Jesus is not only your Savior but as importantly your Lord or leader in every area of your life, then gentleness leans into a spirit of humility that leads to restraint in the way you respond. Those who knew you in the old days wonder what happened to you because of how you used to respond. That's when you have the opportunity to tell them it's all about Jesus.

The idea in the root word for gentleness is the image of a wild stallion with unlimited strength. The bridle controls every movement. The Holy Spirit does that for us. He is our bridle or our guardrail against strength getting out of control in the heat of the moment to the detriment of others.

Paul writes, "Let your gentleness be evident to all. The Lord is near."

PHILIPPIANS 4:5

22

Got a Mountain to Move?

Do you think God has the power to do the impossible? Jesus taught that even small faith, when placed in Him, can accomplish great things through God's strength. It's trusting God to do the impossible according to his perfect will not according to our demand in the moment.

John expressed it in these words: "This is the confidence we have in approaching God: If we ask anything according to his will, he hears us – whatever we ask- we know that we have what we have asked of him" (1 John 5:14-15). According to these verses:

First, **God hears us**. We are not praying into the emptiness of outer space.

Second, **God listens to our prayers**. God knows and cares about our situation or need.

Third, we are to **pray according to God's will**. His will is aligned with his character and the values of his Kingdom.

Fourth, **God moves in response to our prayers** when we come with a surrendered heart that is aligned with his will.

"Do not be conformed to the pattern of this world
but be transformed by the renewing of your mind.
Then you will be able to test and approve what God's will is –
his good, pleasing, and perfect will."

ROMANS 12:2

23

Fearless or Fearful

Courage comes from trusting God. Believers don't need to fear tough times, uncertainty, or past failures because God is with them and strengthens them. David describes it in his most famous psalm, "Even when I walk in death's shadow in the dark valley, I will not be afraid for you are with me and your rod and staff comfort me." Psalm 23:4

What keeps you awake at night? What fear can you turn over to God trusting his presence and strength. It has been said that God is up all night, so you don't have to be! Isaiah understood that truth and captured it in these words for us: "Fear not, for I am with you; be not dismayed, for I am your God."

ISAIAH 41:10

24

Confidence Without Arrogance

Confidence comes from what God does for us not what we do for ourselves. God is in control of his plan for your life when you listen and follow his lead. That means trusting God even when you find yourself on a crooked or broken path: "...being confident of this, that he who began a good work in you will carry it on to completion until the day of Christ Jesus" (Philippians 1:6):

...God started the good work in you, and it doesn't stop there. He will finish it.

...His good work includes salvation, spiritual growth, spiritual gifts, a calling, and empowerment for holy living.

Carrying it on to completion implies that God's work is a life long process that he will never leave incomplete.

...Until the day of Jesus Christ refers to the return of Jesus when God's work will be complete in every believer resulting in spiritual maturity and Christlikeness.

PHILIPPIANS 1:3-6

25

Sticking Close to Jesus

Abiding in Christ means continual dependence, obedience, and following Jesus daily. Then your life will produce the kind of fruit the Spirit makes possible in your life and through your life: love, joy, peace, patience, kindness, goodness, faithfulness, gentleness, and self-control.

> *"Abide in me, and I in you.*
> *As the branch cannot bear fruit by itself...*
> *neither can you, unless you abide in me."*

JOHN 15:4

26

Walking by the Spirit

Walking is the daily activity of moving from one place to another. While you are walking today, live under the Spirit's guidance and power. The Spirit enables believers to resist sin and grow in righteousness while producing spiritual fruit through our life. You walk by the Spirit when you are filled with the Holy Spirit.

Jesus criticized the religious leaders of his day. He called them hypocrites because they looked good on the outside like whitewashed cups, but they were filled with hypocrisy on the inside. When we are forgiven on the inside, then the Holy Spirit can live within us and produce the fruit that represents holy living and presents a holy God to others.

"Walk by the Spirit,
and you will not gratify the desires of the flesh."

GALATIANS 5:16

27

Sometimes a Song Says it Best

Thank You Jesus for the Blood

I was a wretch
I remember who I was
I was lost, I was blind
I was running out of time

Sin separated
The breach was far too wide
But from the far side of the chasm
You held me in your sight

So You made a way
Across the great divide
Left behind Heaven's throne
To build it here inside

And there at the cross
You paid the debt I owed
Broke my chains, freed my soul
For the first time I had hope

You took my place
Laid inside my tomb of sin
You were buried for three days
But then you walked right out again

And now death has no sting
And life has no end
For I have been transformed
By the blood of the lamb

There is nothing stronger
Of the wonder working power of
the blood
That calls us sons and daughters
We are ransomed by the Father
Through the blood

Thank you, Jesus, for the
blood applied
Thank you Jesus, it has washed
me white
Thank you, Jesus, you have saved
my life
Brought me from the darkness
into glorious light[21]

EPHESIANS 1:7

28

Gifted?
Just Do it!

Unlike selfish ambition, followers of Jesus have a holy ambition that seeks God's glory and the advancement of His kingdom. These are God-centered goals that honor him and reflect his calling or prompting in your life.

What has God put in your heart as a "Kingdom Bucket List" item that you would love to be part of? What would you be willing to do for God if there were no limits on you? The Holy Spirit calls out your skills and prompts you to be available for what God has planned for you. The New Testament teaches that God's Holy Spirit equips us for what God wants us to invest in.

"We have different gifts, according to the grace given to each of us. If your gift is prophesying, then prophesy in accordance with your faith; if it is serving, then serve; if it is teaching, then teach; if it is to encourage, then give encouragement; if it is giving, then give generously; if it is to lead, do it diligently; if it is to show mercy, do it cheerfully" (Romans 12:6-8).

Peter says every follower has a gift: "Each of you should use whatever gift you have received to serve others…"

1 PETER 4:10

29

What Is in Store for You

God has blessings in store for you in light of your faithful service. Though salvation is a gift, Scripture promises rewards for obedience, perseverance, and faithfulness. These are blessings given by God for faithful service when he may speak these words: "Well done good and faithful servant" (Matthew 25:23). Your eternal investment today is tomorrow's heavenly reward. One day you will share in God's joy and presence when entering God's eternal Kingdom.

> *"Lay up for yourselves treasures in heaven,*
> *where neither moth nor rust destroys."*

MATTHEW 6:20

30

Running the Race

Life is often a rat-race these days. There is little negotiable time or margin left in our lives once our daily to do list is completed. Persevering in the Christian life is not doing any more in an already overloaded life. It has more to do with how you are going about doing what you already do. It's who you are as you fulfill the responsibilities of today and deal with the stressors and interruptions of your busyness.

The Christian journey requires endurance, discipline, and focus on representing Christ in every conversation and responsibility. Just live your life in a way that reflects how Jesus would do it.

"Let us run with endurance the race that is set before us, looking to Jesus."

HEBREWS 12:1-2

DECEMBER

BUILD
MY LIFE

"You are worthy, our Lord and God,
to receive glory and honor and power,
for you created all things, and by your will
they were created and have their being."

— REVELATION 4:11

Build
My Life

Worthy of every song we could ever sing
Worthy of all the praise we could ever bring
Worthy of every breath we could ever breathe
We live for you

Jesus the Name above every other name
Jesus the only One who could ever save
Worthy of every breath we could ever breathe
We live for you, we live for you

Holy there is no One like you
There is none besides you
Open up my eyes in wonder
Show me who you are
And fill me with your heart
And lead me in your love to those around me

I will build my life upon your love
It is a firm foundation
I will put my trust in you alone
And I will not be shaken[22]

01

Finishing Well

How do you remain faithful all the way to the finish line? A godly finish means holding fast to the faith, fulfilling one's calling, and serving others. It is the ability to get to the end and say, "Thank you Jesus. It wasn't always easy, but following Jesus gave my life meaning and purpose. I am a better person at living my life because of Jesus' teaching and example."

In Paul's final letter before his death, he writes to Timothy, his young protégé. It is an opportunity to reflect on his life and ministry: "I have fought the good fight, I have finished the race, I have kept the faith" (2 Timothy 4:7).

> ...He fought the good fight – His fight was not about people but about spiritual forces, temptation, and sin. He persevered to stay faithful to God's calling and mission (Ephesians 6:2).

> ...He finished the race – It was never about perfection but progress in becoming more like Jesus. He never quit regardless of the hardships he faced along the way (Hebrews 12:1).

> ...He kept the faith – He was a trustee of God's truth without compromising sound doctrine. He taught it. He lived it. He equipped others to follow his lead knowing that his time was short.

Paul believed that finishing well is more important than starting well. His personal mission statement: "Let us not become weary in doing good, for at the proper time we will reap a harvest if we do not give up."

GALATIANS 6:9

02

The 85% Rule

When being right can be wrong...

- Even if you are the smartest one in the room...

- And you are right 85% of the time...

- You can be toxic in your arrogance 15% of the time...

- Sometimes you might just be wrong.

PROVERBS 16:18

03

Need a Light?

Jesus is the light of the world (John 8:12)

Those who follow Christ are no longer living in the darkness of a broken world but are called to walk in his light. Paul understood: "At one time you were darkness, but now you are light...live as children of light" (Ephesians 5:8). It means living in light of God's truth and wisdom. It is knowing, understanding, doing, and becoming what it means to be like Jesus and to live like Jesus.

You are the light of the world (Matthew 5:14)

"You are the light of the world. A town built on a hill cannot be hidden. Neither do people light a lamp and put it under a bowl. Instead, they put it on its stand, and it gives light to everyone in the house. In the same way, let your light shine before others, that they may see your good deeds and glorify your Father in heaven."

How is your light shining? Where is your light shining? Could it be any brighter? Could it stay on longer? Where is you light needed most in your world?

MATTHEW 5:14-16

04

Too Much Salt?

Jesus describes his followers as the salt of the earth who preserve goodness and positively influence the world for good and for God. Salt adds flavor. It preserves from decay. It purifies. It creates thirst.

In the same way, Christians are called to impact society with Christlike living. We are his ambassadors. We may be the only Jesus others may ever see. If you are not salty to your neighbor or co-worker who will be?

Losing your saltiness means losing your distinctiveness by blending into the world instead of influencing it. If you can be both liked and respected, it is a win-win. If you have to choose, choose respect.

"You are the salt of the earth; but if salt has lost its taste, how shall its saltiness be restored?"

MATTHEW 5:13

05

The Foolishness of Listening

The wisdom of the book of Proverbs is its insight into living wisely! Three examples of lousy listeners:

Lousy listening #1 - A fool takes no pleasure in understanding, but only in expressing his opinions" (Proverbs 18:2).

Lousy listening #2 - "If one gives an answer before he hears, it is his folly and shame" (Proverbs 18:13).

Lousy listening #3 - "The way of a fool is right in his own eyes, but a wise man listens to advice."

PROVERBS 12:15

06

Does God Play Favorites?

Can I ask God to let my team win? Does God love me more than my sister? Can I get the most Christmas presents or the biggest raise at work? God does not show favoritism based on status, race, intelligence, or performance:

1. "God does not show partiality" (Romans 2:11).

2. God does choose people for specific purposes in his story – but always to bless others.

3. God demonstrates equal love with unique callings.

4. God's character is perfectly just, fair, and impartial.

Our favoritism says: "I like you best and you deserve special treatment." Favoritism is not fair because I win and you lose.

God's favor says: "I will bless you so you can bless others." Favor comes with responsibility and a call to sacrifice for the benefit of others. We both win.

God loves all people equally: "For God so loved the world…"

JOHN 3:16

07

Who Me, Worry?

Some people are worry-free. Others are worry-some. A few are worry-obsessed.

Worry Free – They can be careless by not worrying reasonably about what might go wrong.

Worry Some – They are the people everyone else worries about because they are accident prone.

Worry Obsessed – They are immobilized in the "what if" trap. Murphy's Law is their continual mindset.

If you get stuck in overthinking every move in your life, remember that worry changes nothing. It is a waste of your time, energy, and emotion.

- Recognize Your Worry – It doesn't help (Matthew 6:27).

- Release Your Worry – Hand it over to God in prayer (Philippians 4:6-7).

- Replace Your Worry – Refocus your thoughts (Philippians 4:8).

Paul's approach: "We take captive every thought to make it obedient to Christ."

2 CORINTHIANS 10:5

08

You Are What You Think

Those attending the Philippian church were challenged to fill their minds with things that lead to worship of God and service to others. Paul understood that we become what we think about and what we focus on: "Finally, brothers and sisters, whatever is true, whatever is noble, whatever is right, whatever is pure, whatever is lovely, whatever is admirable – if anything is excellent or praiseworthy – think about such things" (Philippians 4:8).

True – Does your thinking reflect God's truth or is it your assumption or what others are saying?

Noble – Does your thinking lift you up or depress?

Right – Does your thinking reflect God's righteousness of living in right relationships with others?

Pure – Is your thinking morally and ethically clean?

Lovely – Does your thinking lead you toward love, grace, and peace?

Admirable – Does your thinking contribute to your positive reputation if known to everyone?

Excellent – Does your thinking move you from settling for what is to growing into Christlikeness?

Praiseworthy – Is your thinking pleasing in the mind of God who knows everything about you?

Paul adds his own example in the next verse: "What you have learned and received, and heard, and seen in me – practice these things, and the God of peace will be with you."

PHILIPPIANS 4:9

09

Identity or Reputation

Identity is what we think about ourselves in light of our intentions. Reputation is what other people think about us in light of our observed behavior. "A good name is more desirable than great riches; to be esteemed is better than silver or gold" (Proverbs 22:1).

Sometimes we don't see ourselves in the same way other people do. Two pathways to healthy honesty and self-understanding:

Giving Others Feedback About Yourself - Opening up the hidden areas of our life to a few trusted friends brings accountability for the areas where we need further growth. Rober Boyd Munger's classic devotional is all about opening up. *My Heart-Christ's Home* is a simple but powerful metaphor of the heart pictured as a house to illustrate what it means to welcome Jesus into every area of our lives. It opens the doors of our life from the public living room to the hidden rooms behind locked doors. How open are you?

Receiving Others' Feedback About You – Accepting what a few trusted others see as our blind spots in character and personality is wise and biblical. It reflects the truth in Proverbs 27:17 that "Iron sharpens iron." Growth comes through the counsel and correction of others. Choose people who will be honest more than polite, who are spiritually mature and grounded in God's truth. Choose those who are courageous enough to tell you what you may not want to hear, and those who are genuinely committed to investing in your personal growth.

"Whoever heeds life-giving correction will be at home among the wise."

PROVERBS 15:31

10

Jesus the Amazing Scientist

Science tells us that we need four basics to survive: water, air, food, and light.

1. Jesus told the woman at the will that he offers living water. (John 4:10-14)

2. Jesus breathes life into his followers when his breath imparted the Holy Spirit on his followers. (John 20:22)

3. Jesus referred to himself as the bread of life. (John 6:35)

4. Jesus spoke to the people and said: "I am the light of the world." (John 0:12)

No wonder the writer of Psalm 23 says, "The Lord is my shepherd. I have everything I need."

PSALM 23:1

11

The Bad Archer

The Hebrew word for sin, *hata*, and the Greek word for sin, *hamartia*, literally mean to miss the mark. It is the same word used in archery when the arrow fails to hit its target.

In God's eyes, sin isn't just doing something bad, it is missing God's intended mark for your life. Sometimes we settle for the outer ring on the target of life when God wants us to hit his bull's eye.

Are you missing the mark in God's plan and purpose for your life by aiming at your own target, in your own ways, to your own benefit rather than to the benefit of others?

ROMANS 3:23

12

Want Advice?
Really?

"Listen to advice and accept discipline, and at the end you will be counted among the wise" (Proverbs 19:20). With most you will often have to ask insightful questions in order to get their honest advice. Only ask trusted friends who consistently model the best of Christlike maturity.

Question #1 – What three words describe how others see me?

Question #2 – What strengths do you see in me that I may not yet see?

Question #3 – What one behavior would enhance my interpersonal skills contributing to my relationships and my witness for Christ?

Question #4 – Have you seen evidence of spiritual growth in my life? Do you have a recommendation of where I should grow more?

Question #5 – Is there any part of my life where God is waiting for me to surrender to him?

Listen without defending. Pray over what you have heard. Act on what you hear. "Instruct the wise and they will be wiser still."

PROVERBS 9:9

13

God's Eternal Guest List

The Book of Life is God's record of who is in and those who chose to stay out.

- **It's about belonging.** It symbolizes being known by God as his own.

- **It's about security.** Being included in the Book of Life points to eternal life through Christ.

- **It's about a warning.** Those who reject God risk being left out.

- **It's about hope.** It assures believers of final salvation and eternal fellowship with God.

Jesus promises: "I will never blot out the name of the one who is victorious from the book of life."

REVELATION 3:5

14

The White Throne Judgment

The final judgment before God's throne is called The White Throne Judgment in Revelation 20:11-15.

All the dead, great and small, will stand before God to be judged according to their deeds and their response to Christ. It is a day of eternal accountability. The scene represents the ultimate and universal judgment of humanity after the final resurrection. God's Book of Life represents the record of your life, your every thought, and your every action. Every day is preparation for that day. Every attitude. Every word. Every act.

> *"Then I saw a great white throne*
> *and him who was seated on it...*
> *and the dead were judged by*
> *what was written in the books."*

REVELATION 20:11-12

15

New Heavens and New Earth

After God's final judgment, he will establish a new, perfect world free from sin, pain, and death. God will dwell with his people is in this renewed creation.

- **In the Old Testament**, the Prophet Isaiah records God's promise: "See, I will create new heavens and a new earth. The former things will not be remembered, nor will they come to mind" (Isaiah 65:17; 66:22).

- **In the New Testament**, John's vision includes this picture: "Then I saw a new heaven and a new earth, for the first heaven and the first earth had passed away, and there was no longer any sea" (Revelation 21:1). Sorry to all "anglers." It sounds like fishing is out in eternity!

The new heaven and the new earth is all about restoration, not destruction. God is redeeming and renewing everything broken by sin. The new creation will be free from sin, corruption, and death. God will be present with his people. History is always moving toward God's good and glorious future. Peter commented: "But in keeping with his promise we are looking forward to a new heaven and a new earth, where righteousness dwells."

2 PETER 3:13

16

Tree of Life

The Tree of Life is one of the most powerful biblical images, mentioned in Genesis and then in the last book in the Bible. It is the symbol of eternal life with God.

After Adam and Eve sinned, access to the Tree of Life was blocked to prevent eternal life in a fallen state (Genesis 3:22-24). It was lost to humanity in the Garden of Eden, but the Tree of Life reappears in the new creation as a source of healing and life (Revelation 22:1-2, 14). What was lost in Eden is regained in Christ's second coming. God is renewing his original plan for all of creation.

> *"The tree of life with its twelve kinds of fruit,*
> *yielding its fruit each month.*
> *The leaves of the tree were for*
> *the healing of the nations."*

REVELATION 22:2

17

River of Life

This biblical image symbolizes God's eternal refreshment and blessing for healing and renewal. The tree runs through Jerusalem with the Tree of Life on either side, and its waters bring healing to the nations.

The river originates from God's throne, showing that all life flows from him. It represents spiritual renewal and eternal joy. Wherever the river flows it replaces brokenness and death with wholeness and life.

John's vision includes this: "The river of the water of life, bright as crystal, flowing from the throne of God and of the Lamb."

REVELATION 22:1

18

A New Heavenly Jerusalem

It is the eternal city of God's redeemed people described as a radiant city where God dwells with His people forever. It's not just a place but it includes the restored relationship between God and his people. Unlike the old Jerusalem, which was bound by earthly limitations and failures, the new Jerusalem is eternal, holy, and radiant with God's glory.

...No temple is needed because God himself and the Lamb (Christ) are its temple, Revelation 21:22.

...No suffering as every tear will be wiped from their eyes, Revelation 21:4

...Radiance and Purity are everywhere as the city shines with the glory of God.

...Living Water and Tree of Life as the water flows from the throne.

The New Jerusalem is a picture of hope and renewal as God's Covenant is fulfilled for all eternity.

"I saw the holy city, new Jerusalem,
coming down out of heaven from God,
prepared as a bride adorned for her husband."

REVELATION 21:2

19

No More Tears

Regardless of the pain and suffering on earth, the New Heaven and the New Earth will be the end of sorrow and suffering in God's kingdom.

God promises to wipe away every tear, removing death, mourning, pain, and loss forever.

"He will wipe away every tear from their eyes, and death shall be no more."

REVELATION 21:4

20

Eternal Glory

In eternity we share in Christ's resurrection, victory over sin and death, and participation in his reign. God's Glory follows our perseverance as suffering leads to honor in God's Kingdom. Unlike earthly recognition or fading achievements, eternal glory never diminishes. It points to the believer's destiny of being fully restored in God's presence.

Suffering in this life is temporary and cannot compare with the glory awaiting believers in eternity, so Paul says: "This light and momentary affliction is preparing for us an eternal weight of glory beyond all comparison."

2 CORINTHIANS 4:17

21

Everlasting Joy

There is unending gladness found in God's presence. Joy will replace sorrow completely in God's kingdom, as his people rejoice forever. Heaven is a place where the fulfillment of God's promise of hope and optimism dominates every moment. Want to be happy forever? Better yet, want to have eternal joy? I look forward to meeting for some angelic laughter, hopefully with a cup of coffee and a heavenly cinnamon roll at the Main Street Cafe in heaven! No more calorie-counting there!

The Old Testament Prophet looked forward to this new day: "The ransomed of the Lord shall return and come to Zion with singing; everlasting joy shall be upon their heads."

ISAIAH 35:10

22

Hope of Our Resurrection

Our everlasting hope is the assurance that believers will rise from the dead when Christ returns. His resurrection guarantees that his people will also be raised, trans- formed, and given a new heavenly body for eternal life. It is one of the central promises of the Christian faith. The resurrection of Jesus is the foundation of Christian hope.

It' personal. The anticipation of life after death.

It's cosmic. The anticipation of the renewal of all creation.

It's biblical. The anticipation that, "The dead will be raised imperishable, and we shall be changed."

1 CORINTHIANS 15:52

23

Final Victory

The victory is Christ's ultimate triumph over sin, death, Satan, and all things evil. History is moving toward a decisive moment when Christ will return, evil will be judged, and God's people will share in his eternal reign. God's final victory includes:

Christ's resurrection as the cornerstone of all we hope for. It guarantees the final victory over sin and death.

Defeat of evil is the day the world has been waiting for.

Fulfillment of God's Kingdom when God establishes a new heaven and new earth.

Eternal assurance where believer's hope is fulfilled knowing that suffering, sin, and sorrow will not have the final word.

The cross and resurrection secured God's victory, and at the end of time this victory will be fully revealed.

> *"Thanks be to God, who gives us the victory through our Lord Jesus Christ."*

1 CORINTHIANS 15:57

24

It's Christmas Eve

"The people walking in great darkness have seen a great light...For unto us a child is born, to us a son is given, and the government will be on his shoulders...Of the greatness of his government and peace there will be no end. He will reign on David's throne and over his kingdom, establishing and upholding it with justice and righteousness from that time on and forever. The zeal of the Lord Almighty will accomplish this" (Isaiah 9:2, 6-7).

The prophet Isaiah wrote these prophetic words more than 700 years before Jesus was born. He spoke into a world of darkness—one filled with conflict, confusion, and fear. His words reached a people who had lost their way living in exile while waiting for a sign that God had not forgotten them.

Christmas Eve reminds us that this prophecy was fulfilled through the birth of Jesus Christ. The light Isaiah saw entered the world, not through power or prestige, but through a baby born in Bethlehem. Jesus is our Wonderful Counselor who brings wisdom to our confusion, our Mighty God who overcomes our weakness, our Everlasting Father who loves with perfect care, and our Prince of Peace who calms in every storm.

ISAIAH 9:6

25

It's Christmas Day

"But you, Bethlehem Ephrathah, though you are small among the clans of Judah, out of you will come for me one who will be ruler over Israel, whose origins are from old, from ancient times. Therefore, Israel will be abandoned until the time when she who is in labor bears a son...he will stand and shepherd his flock in the strength of the Lord his God" (Micah 5:2-4).

Micah's prophetic words were also written more than 700 years before the birth of Jesus in the little town of Bethlehem! It was a time without hope, yet God chose to speak words of hope through his promised and anticipated actions. The fulfillment of God's promise would come from the hometown of King David where, one day, another "Shepherd King" like David would be born whose reign would extend to the ends of the earth.

This prophecy reminds us that God works through the small, insignificant, and often overlooked. The Savior of the world did not come from a palace or capital city, but from a humble town, through a young woman's and young man's obedience, and into a dark world needing light. That light is still needed today.

1 SAMUEL 17:12

26

The story of Christmas Is as easy as 1, 2, 3

It begins with childlike simplicity:

> **One** baby enters the world

> **Two** parents say yes to God

> **Three** shepherds run toward new hope

It continues with worshipping visitors:

> **One** star breaks the darkness

> **Two** years pass on the calendar

> **Three** wise men bow in worship

The story turns dark:

> **One** betrayed arrest

> **Two** false witnesses

> **Three** crosses on a hill

The story goes silent:

> **One** woman comes to grieve

> **Two** angels speak of hope

> **Three** days later the tomb is empty

The story reaches us:

> **One** Savior – Jesus

> **Two** choices – follow Jesus or walk away

> **Three** invitations – Ask. Seek. Knock.

MATTHEW 7:7-8

27

In Heaven's Name
What Do Angels Do?

Angels are created spiritual beings who serve God and carry out his will in both the heavenly and earthly realms. Their ministry includes provision (1 Kings 19:5-7), guidance (Acts 8:26), protection (Daniel 6:22), judgment (Genesis 19), and encouragement (Luke 22:43).

For humans, angels are messengers and ministers sent to protect, guide, and serve believers as well. Angels also battle spiritual forces of evil (Daniel 10:12-13; Revelation 12:7-9.).

"Are they not all ministering spirits sent out to serve for the sake of those who are to inherit salvation?"

HEBREWS 1:14

28

Living Today While
Waiting for Tomorrow

How do you balance the demands of today while living with the expectation of a better eternal day coming?

1. The Bible affirms planning yet warns against overconfidence about the future. So, plan wisely, but hold plans lightly with humility (Proverbs 16:3, 9; James 4:13-15).

2. Jesus repeatedly emphasized living in the present moment rather than living in yesterday or only living for tomorrow. We are given grace for today (Matthew 6:34; Psalm 118:24).

3. Trust God with what is not certain or out of your control. God is already in the future preparing the way for each of our next steps (1 Peter 5:7; Proverbs 3:5-6).

4. Remember God's faithfulness in the past. He does what he promises, and he doe not change (Psalm 77:11; Hebrews 13:8).

5. Be mindful of eternity while living faithfully today in light of tomorrow. God takes the long view, not for us to escape the present day, but to live purposefully today (Colossians 3:2; Psalm 90:12).

6. Jesus taught that how we live now prepares us for what is ahead. God uses today to shape you for the future he's leading you into (Matthew 25:14-30; Luke 16:10).

> *"We fix our eyes...on what is unseen,*
> *since what is seen is temporary."*

2 CORINTHIANS 4:18

29

How to Deal with a Prodigal?

When a child, spouse, sibling, or friend is a prodigal, it can be emotionally exhausting and spiritually stretching. Luke 15:11-32 pictures the prodigal as someone who rejects God's wisdom, walks away from God and sometimes from family, and chooses a path of self-destruction.

- The father in the parable never stopped loving his son, even though he did not chase after him. Guard your heart from bitterness or self-blame. Pray for a compassionate spirit of mercy and grace rather than self-righteous judgment.

- Tough love never enables destructive behavior or our felt need to protect them from the consequences of their choices. Set clear boundaries for yourself while speaking the truth in grace. God allows the natural consequences of our decisions to be our most effective teachers.

- Keep the door unlocked and keep the light on without trying to force reconciliation. Never plead or emotionally pressure the prodigal. The father just kept watching from a distance.

- Pray for a wake-up call (Luke 15:17). Prodigals often return when they know they will be welcomed in grace. Prepare for their return and allow time for trust to be restored.

- Have the party supplies ready or reservations made to celebrate when the prodigal returns home.

God doesn't categorize prodigals in term of good or bad but in terms of lost or found. See Jesus' three parables in Luke 15:3-32.

LUKE 15:20

30

Victory of the Lamb

This phrase points to Jesus Christ's triumph through his death and resurrection. It emphasizes that Christ, the sacrificial Lamb of God, won the battle over sin, death, Satan, and evil. He did this not through earthly power but through his humility, sacrifice, and obedience to his Heavenly Father.

The Second Coming will be Christ's final triumph:

- **Over Sin** – His sacrifice satisfied justice and brought forgiveness, (Romans 8:1-3).

- **Over Death** – His resurrection broke the power of the grave, (1 Corinthians 15:54-57).

- **Over Satan** – By the cross, Jesus disarmed the powers of evil, (Colossians 2:15).

Jesus, the Lamb of God, defeats all powers of darkness, and His followers share in His victory. "The Lamb will conquer them, for he is Lord of lords and King of kings."

REVELATION 17:14

31

The End Is Just
the Beginning

"Forget the former things; do not dwell on the past. See, I am doing a new thing! Now it springs up; do you not perceive it? I am making a way in the wilderness and streams in the wasteland" (Isaiah 43:18-19).

God promises renewal even when something else ends. He is already at work creating something new in you. The "way in the wilderness" symbolizes direction where there was none. Transformation often begins in the wilderness – the place of endings and uncertainty and then new beginnings.

If you picked up this book in a season of doubt, deconstruction, or disappointment with the church, with Christians, or with God, I honor your courage. As you reach the end of these 365 days, my prayer is that this journey has provided an overview of the Bible to help you see Jesus with fresh eyes and renewed hope. Faith is not a destination you achieve—it is a relationship you cultivate with a daily invitation to walk alongside the One who promised to never to leave you (John 14:18).

May your questions lead to deeper truth. May the truth you've discovered draw you closer to the heart of Jesus. May Jesus be the cornerstone of the faith you are reconstructing. Continue seeking, listening, and trusting. He is nearer than you think—and far better than you ever imagined. The world is aching for people who actually live the Jesus' way. May you be one of them. Amen, so let it be true.

Whoever follows me will not walk in darkness,
but will have the light of life.

JOHN 8:12

*"...choose this day whom you will serve.
But as for me and my house,
we will serve the Lord."*

— JOSHUA 24:15

RECONSTRUCTING FAITH

The Jesus Way

If you curse me, then I will bless you
If you hurt me, I will forgive
And if you hate me, then I will love you
I choose the Jesus way

If you're helpless, I will defend you
And if you're burdened, I'll share the weight
And if you're hopeless, then let me show you
There's hope in the Jesus way

If you strike me, I will embrace you
And if you chain me, I'll sing his praise
And if you kill me, my home is heaven
For I choose the Jesus way

I follow Jesus
He wore my sin, I'll gladly wear his name
He is the treasure
He is the answer
Oh, I choose the Jesus way
And I choose surrender
I choose to love
Oh, God my Savior, you'll always be enough
I choose forgiveness
I choose grace
I choose to worship, no matter what I face
I follow Jesus
He wore my sin, I'll gladly wear his name
He is the treasure
He is the answer
Oh, I choose the Jesus way[23]

AFTERWORD

THE BIBLE IS THE unfolding story of God's relentless pursuit to restore a broken relationship that sin damaged between us and a Holy God. That story was written by forty authors over fifteen centuries, on three continents, and in three languages, and it continues today with one central theme: The retelling of what happens when the God of Heaven steps into our time in history to offer forgiveness and reconciliation in a renewed relationship with him.

For that reason alone, consider the impact this record of God's love for a lost and broken world has had:

» The Bible is the most printed, most translated, and most enduring book in human history—now available in more than 3,600 languages, with over 5 billion copies in circulation.

» The wisdom of God contained in its pages has shaped law, ethics, literature, art, and culture across generations and continents.

» The eyewitness accounts of Jesus' death and resurrection record the central truth of faith for more than 2.5 billion believers around the world.

» Despite repeated attempts through history to ban, burn, distort, or destroy it, the Bible still stands—unchanged and unbroken.

The Old Testament tells the story of God's original covenant. It is his agreement with Israel including his laws to protect them, his promises to inspire them, and his faithfulness to lead them across the generations of human history.

The New Testament reveals the fulfillment of those promises in Jesus Christ as God's forever plan of salvation for all people. The Old Testament provides context and prophecy; the New Testament proclaims the fulfillment of that prophecy in the redemption of lost people through Christ.

The Bible's message for the twenty-first century remains timeless and personal: an invitation to follow Jesus. He is the only God among all religions who comes to us rather than asking us to find our way to him. He knows us, he loves us, and he finds us. He is the only God who chooses to die for those he loves—paying the debt for our sin and offering forgiveness that leads to a new way of living, an other-centered way of living.

When we look at our own lives and the world we live in, we may wonder why God allows suffering. The story of Scripture reminds us that the one who suffered the worst imaginable pain and rejection and humiliation was the best possible person in all of human history. He got what he didn't deserve but what God had planned to save the world from their sin.

Suffering is a part of our human story in a broken and sinful world. Suffering is also part of God's story to fix what is broken in us and in our world. Jesus willingly died on a cross to reconcile you to God. He lives today to guide you through the wisdom of his teaching, and he offers us the Holy Spirit living within us to empower us for holy living.

Jesus' example and teaching upended a centuries-old, self-centered way of living for personal gain, community status, selfish power, and the comforts of privilege. When Jesus calls us to an other-centered life, it is a life of humility, service, sacrifice, of lifting others up. The world says, "Use people to get ahead." The Jesus' way says, "Use your power to help others move ahead."

In some of Jesus' final teaching moments with his followers, he left this thought lingering in their minds just before the events of his arrest, trial, crucifixion, and resurrection. "You know that the rulers of the Gentiles lord it over them...Not so with you. Instead, whoever wants to become great among you must be your servant, and whoever wants to be first must be your slave" (Matthew 20:25-27).

Think of what that kind of living and leading would look like in your family. In your workplace. In your church. In your community. In our world.

What? So What? Now What?

What stands between you and Jesus?

Be honest with yourself.

Be honest about it with God.

Accept God's offer of forgiveness.

Make things right with other people.

Follow Jesus' teaching and his example.

Tell your God story and live your God story.

Live a life more for other people than for yourself.

Anticipate your eternity in God's presence ... forever.

*"Praise be to the God and Father of our lord Jesus Christ!
In his great mercy he has given us new birth into a living hope
through the resurrection of Jesus Christ from the dead."*

1 PETER 1:3

"Jesus performed many other signs in the presence of his disciples, which are not recorded in this book. But these are written that you may believe that Jesus is the Messiah, the Son of God, and that by believing you may have life in his name."

JOHN 20:30-31

ACKNOWLEDGEMENTS

I AM GRATEFUL TO Heidi Sheard for her exceptional editorial expertise and thoughtful guidance throughout the development of this manuscript. This project adds to four previous books that Heidi has assisted with. Each one ends up with greater clarity and is more concise thanks to her skills in refining and enhancing words, sentences, paragraphs, and entire books! She always keeps the reader in mind while protecting my intention in the thoughts that translate into words on each page.

Thank you as well to Kendal Marsh for contributing his creative talent to the cover design and interior layout, helping bring the book to life visually. This is our fifth writing project together. Each one builds on the previous to create visual continuity with creativity in the visual icon identified for each book. People who give me feedback on this collection often refer to the interior design that surprised me in the very first book. I was delighted with his way of arranging the entire book as well as each page.

I know I am very blessed by family roots with parents who were followers of Jesus. They modeled Jesus' teaching as much in their walk as in their talk. My siblings continue to join me on this journey of faith in this senior season of life. Most importantly, I am inspired by my three adult children and seven grandchildren, who continue in their busiest season of life to regularly invest family time in communities of faith in their neighborhoods. That legacy outshines anything else I might accomplish.

I also acknowledge the valuable support of ChatGPT, which assisted with content refinement and development during the writing process.

ABOUT THE AUTHOR

DR. DICK DANIELS is the Founder and President of The Leadership Development Group, established in 2008. He also leads a global LinkedIn community by the same name, consisting of more than 275,000 leadership practitioners who collaborate daily on the real-world challenges of leading and developing people at every level. Previously, Daniels served as Dean of Student Development at Bethel Theological Seminary, where he launched the Association for Student Development in Theological Education and hosted three national conferences focused on nurturing the personal and spiritual growth of future ministry leaders. He has also been a church planter, launching congregations in Phoenix and Minneapolis.

Daniels is the author of four nationally awarded leadership books in The Leadership Development Group library (www.The365DayLeader.org), and four children's titles in the Oak Street Treehouse series—which have also earned national book awards (www.OakStreetTreehouse.com). His proudest accomplishment, however, is his family: three adult children and seven grandchildren.

For more than twenty years, Daniels has served as an Executive Leadership Development Coach for corporate leaders across industries. He is a Certified Master Coach with Marshall Goldsmith's Stakeholder Centered Coaching and partners with the Chief Executive Group as both an executive coach and a recurring facilitator for Chief Executive Network events.

Daniels invests in the next generation through his volunteer work with Young Life in Naples, Florida, including their Capernaum Club for students with special needs—where he helped launch a Capernaum Choir. Internationally, he serves with Young Life Nordic, supporting high school camps in Norway and Sweden as a Work Crew volunteer.

ABOUT THE BOOK

RECONSTRUCTING FAITH grew out of Dick Daniels' decades of serving and working in local churches, theological education, and more recently in corporate executive coaching in a great variety of industry sectors. He's walked with people of deep faith, people who once believed but drifted away, and people who have never been sure what they think about God at all. Their questions, struggles, answers, and hopes shaped this book.

This is an invitation to take a fresh look at Jesus—the central figure of the Christian story—one short daily reading at a time. Christians believe that God stepped into human history and absorbed the cost of human sin through the sinless life, sacrificial death, and resurrection of Jesus Christ. The New Testament writings come from those who knew him firsthand. They wrestled with doubts, saw the extraordinary up close, and ultimately gave their lives to advance a movement that has reached every continent and every culture. Jesus' call is both simple and profound: "Follow me." Follow his example. Follow his teaching. Follow the one who walked through the same kind of world we do.

Following Jesus is always a choice—your choice. This year-long journey gives you the time and space to honestly explore who Jesus claimed to be and what that might mean for your life. There's no hidden code to crack—just an invitation into a way of living that is radically other-centered in a world that encourages us to be obsessed with self.

Let's reconsider Jesus together. Then you decide where that leads!

ENDNOTES

1   Terry Borton, Reach, Touch, and Teach: Student Concerns and Process Education (McGraw Hill, 1970), 79.

2   "In Christ Alone," words by Stuart Townend and music by Keith Getty, © 2001 Thankyou Music (PRS), administered worldwide at CapitolCMGPublishing. com, excluding Europe which is administered by IntegrityMusic.com.

3   "No Other King," by Mitch Wong, Chris Renzema, and Patrick Mayberry, performed by North Point Worship (Centricity Music/Integrity Music, 2022).

4   "Holy Forever," by Jenn Johnson, Brian Johnson, Chris Tomlin, Jason Ingram, and Phil Wickham (Bethel Music Publishing, Be Essential Songs, Capitol CMG Paragon, Essential Music Publishing, 2022).

5   "I Believe You," by Colby Wedgeworth, Ethan Gregory Hulse, and Megan Woods (Capitol CMG/Bethel Music Publishing, 2018).

6   "Goodness of God," by Jenn Johnson, Ed Cash, Jason Ingram, Ben Fielding, and Brian Johnson (Bethel Music Publishing/Essential Music Publishing, 2018).

7   "All people that on earth do dwell," by William Kethe (Geneva, 1561), www. hymnologyarchive.com/all-people-that-on-earth, accessed October 8, 2025.

8   "How Great Is Our God," by Chris Tomlin, Ed Cash, and Jesse Reeves (sixsteps Music, worshiptogether.com Songs, Wondrously Made Songs, EMI CMG Publishing, 2004).

9   "What a Beautiful Name," by Benjamin David Fielding and Brooke Ligertwood, performed by Hillsong Worship (Hillsong Music Publishing, 2016).

10 "The Prayer," by Carole Bayer Sager and David Foster, performed by Celine Dion and Andrea Bocelli (Warner-Barham Music LLC/Universal Music Publishing, Columbia/Epic, 1998).

11 "The Blessing," by Christopher Joel Brown, Steven Furtick, Cody Carnes, and Kari Brooke Jobe, performed by Elevation Worship (Elevation Worship Publishing, Capitol CMG Paragon, Be Essential Songs, Kari Jobe Carnes Music, Writer's Roof Publishing, Worship Together Music, 2020).

12 "The Church," by Jenn Johnson, David Funk, Oscar Gamboa, Gabriel Gamboa, Julian Gamboa, Sebastian Suarez, Abbie Gamboa, Elyssa Smith, and Kristian Stanfill, performed by Bethel Music (Bethel Music Publishing, 2025).

13 "Johannes Kepler, 'Thinking God's Thoughts After Him,'" BreakPoint, November 26, 2023, www.breakpoint.org/johannes-kepler-thinking-gods-thoughts-after-him/, accessed October 30, 2025".

14 "Look Up Child," by Lauren Daigle, Bebo Norman, Jason Ingram, Mike Donehey, and Paul Brendon Mabury, performed by Lauren Daigle (Centricity Music, 2018).

15 "You Are My King (Amazing Love)," by Billy James Foote (worshiptogether. com Songs/EMI CMG Publishing, 1999).

16 "The Old Rugged Cross," by George Bennard (1913).

17 "Living Hope," by Phil Wickham and Brian Johnson(Phil Wickham Music, Simply Global Songs, Sing My Songs, Bethel Music Publishing, 2018).

18 Timothy Keller, The New City Catechism: 52 Questions and Answers for Our Hearts and Minds (Wheaton, IL: Crossway, 2017).

19 "Made for More," by Josh Baldwin, Jesse Early, Jonathan Smith, and Blake Wiggins (Bethel Music Publishing, 2024).

20 Ann Voskamp, *One Thousand Gifts: A Dare to Live Fully Right Where You Are* (Grand Rapids, MI: Zondervan, 2010).

21 "Thank You Jesus for the Blood," by Charity Gayle, Ryan Kennedy, Steven Musso, David Gentiles, and Bryan McCleery (Gather House Music, Watershed Worship Publishing, McCleery MSC, Come Up Kings Publishing, Steven Musso Music, Centricity Music Publishing, 2021).

22 "Build My Life," by Pat Barrett, Brett Younker, Karl Martin, Kirby Kaple, and Matt Redman (Kaple Music, Capitol CMG Publishing, Housefires Sounds, Said And Done Music, sixsteps Music, ThankYou Music, worshiptogether.com songs, 2018).

23 "The Jesus Way," by Phil Wickham and Jonathan Smith (Phil Wickham Music, Simply Global Songs, Cashagamble Jet Music, Be Essential Songs, 2023).

TOPIC REFERENCE GUIDE

unashamed, 281
unbroken, 423
unchanging, 42, 266
unclean, 151
uncomfortable, 9
undefiled, 367
underrated, 36
unending gladness, 408
unexpected, 215
unfailing love, 171, 364
unfairness, 9
unfaithfulness, 201, 224, 236
unhurried time, 127
uninterrupted, 200
uniqueness, 137, 326
unites, 344, 361
uniting, 81, 276
unity, 97, 99, 117, 136, 197, 262, 282, 285, 312, 359, 366
unnoticed, 32, 163, 302
unpredictability, 37
unrepentant, 167
unresolved, 338
unrighteousness, 144
unshakable, 238, 266
unsure, 19, 61

V
victims, 311
victory, 17, 23, 166, 237, 284, 304, 309, 317, 333, 352, 355, 407, 410, 417
violence, 311
vision, 35, 101, 103, 136, 138, 151, 224, 235–36, 336
vows, 203
vulnerable, 315, 367

W
wandering, 81
war, 60, 166, 283–84, 352
weakness, 64, 115, 191, 193, 219, 262, 309–10, 411

weary, 160, 388
wholeness, 219, 231, 404
widows, 67, 258, 367–68
wilderness wandering, 292
willpower, 259, 335
wisdom, 179, 212
wishful thinking, 86, 186
wit, 53, 61
witnesses, 45, 67, 69, 78, 97, 126, 153, 203, 227, 305, 366, 399, 413
woman, 64, 80, 150, 163, 349, 372, 397, 412-13
womb, 137, 295
women, 45, 64, 138, 304, 367
women in new testament leadership, 305
women in the church, 64
work, 10, 32, 100, 102, 117–18, 127–28, 203, 206–7, 235, 256–57, 259, 261, 289, 355, 357–58
work of christ, 83, 85
workplace, 424
works, 132, 178
world, 119, 327, 365
worry, 50, 394
worship, 12, 61, 67, 89, 134, 163, 165, 201, 204, 212, 234, 263, 275–76, 283, 285-86, 290, 293, 339–47, 413, 421, 430
woundedness, 358

Y
yahweh, 145-6, 161
yoke, 244
yom kippur, 292

Z
zebedee, 162
zechariah, 108, 236
zephaniah, 236
zion, 408
zophar, 95

THE LEADERSHIP DEVELOPMENT GROUP LIBRARY

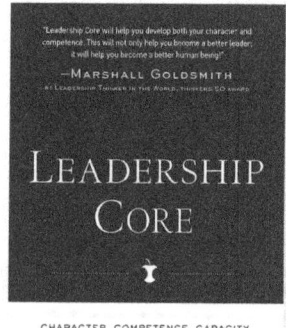

The OakStreet TREEHOUSE Series

A snapshot of God
for your children and grandchildren

God Made Everything
#1 The Day They Messaged God

God Loves Everybody
#2 The Day The New Kid Moved In

God is the Host of Heaven
#3 The Day They Had A Party

God Came & Lived Next Door
#4 The Day They Played Christmas

Visit oakstreettreehouse.com
or scan the code
for books, coloring pages,
and discussion tips!